done in a day
Garden Projects

done in a day
Garden Projects

STEWART WALTON

TIME®
LIFE
BOOKS

Alexandria, Virginia

TIME LIFE BOOKS

TIME-LIFE BOOKS IS A DIVISION OF TIME LIFE INC.

TIME LIFE INC.
PRESIDENT AND CEO: GEORGE ARTANDI
TIME-LIFE CUSTOM PUBLISHING
VICE PRESIDENT AND PUBLISHER: TERRY NEWELL
VICE PRESIDENT OF SALES AND MARKETING: NEIL LEVIN
DIRECTOR OF SPECIAL SALES: LIZ ZIEHL
DIRECTOR OF ACQUISITIONS: JENNIFER PEARCE
PROJECT MANAGER: JENNIE HALFANT

TIME-LIFE IS A TRADEMARK OF TIME WARNER INC. U.S.A.

LIBRARY OF CONGRESS CATALOGING-IN-PUBLICATION DATA
WALTON, STEWART.
    GARDEN PROJECTS / BY STEWART WALTON.
        P. CM. -- (DONE IN A DAY)
    INCLUDES INDEX
    ISBN 0-7835-5310-2 (ALK. PAPER)
    1. GARDEN STRUCTURES -- AMATEURS' MANUALS. I. TITLE. II. SERIES:
WALTON, STEWART.   DONE IN A DAY
TH4961.W35 1998
684.1'.8--DC21   98-28747
                                                        CIP
A MARSHALL EDITION. CONCEIVED, EDITED, AND DESIGNED BY MARSHALL
EDITIONS LTD
THE ORANGERY, 161 NEW BOND STREET LONDON W1Y 9PA

FIRST PUBLISHED IN THE UK IN 1998 BY MARSHALL PUBLISHING LTD
COPYRIGHT © 1998 MARSHALL EDITIONS DEVELOPMENTS LTD
ALL RIGHTS RESERVED INCLUDING THE RIGHT OF REPRODUCTION IN WHOLE OR
IN PART IN ANY FORM

PROJECT EDITOR: ESTHER LABI
DESIGNER: BRIDGEWATER BOOKS
CONSULTANT: SALLY WALTON
PHOTOGRAPHER: GRAHAM RAE
ILLUSTRATOR: KUO KANG CHEN
ART DIRECTOR: SEAN KEOGH
DTP EDITOR: LESLEY GILBERT
MANAGING EDITOR: CLARE CURRIE
EDITORIAL COORDINATOR: REBECCA CLUNES
PRODUCTION: JAMES BANN

ORIGINATED IN SINGAPORE BY MASTER IMAGE   PRINTED AND BOUND IN ITALY

CONTENTS

INTRODUCTION

Does your backyard consist solely of an expanse of grass and a few paving stones or shrubs? Perhaps you'd like to liven up your garden, patio, or roof terrace, but don't know where to start? Within these pages you'll find twelve exciting, inspirational garden features that will help you turn your backyard into a vibrant outdoor living area.

If you are planning a garden from scratch, focus on one or more of the garden projects, and design your garden around it (several projects would easily work together in one garden, depending on its size). If your garden is already established, you can adapt one of the projects to suit your own requirements. You may find it easier to reach for a pencil to sketch out your design before you reach for your tools. Watch the garden at different times of the day—what is the hottest part of the garden? Will any areas get winter sun? It is also worth investing in a soil tester and making a list of plants that are suitable for your soil type. Once you have decided what plants are going in your garden, you have to work out how to best display them.

There are projects that will appeal to the do-it-yourself novice and expert alike. If you are not very confident with wood-working techniques, try the **water feature**, a simple pond that involves very simple but effective tiling. If you don't want to try your hand at tiling, take a look at the homemade hammock—there's no sewing involved at all. Imagine lying next to your water feature, in your hammock—a picture of tranquility! If you've never tried bricklaying before, why not follow the easy steps and build a **brick barbecue** or a **raised herb bed**. Let all the family join in—you can use the herbs in marinades for the food for the barbecue, which the family is sure to enjoy.

Kids love to get involved in the garden, whether it's making mud pies in the boat-shaped **seaside sandbox** or growing seedlings and watching them bloom in **a perfect window box**. The **picnic table and seats** is another project that they can get involved in making—they'll love helping you paint it in bright colors.

If you enjoy watching wildlife, particularly birds, encourage them to feed in your garden by building the **rotund bird feeder**, which can be placed on a pedestal or hung from a tree. Make or buy ready-made birdseed cakes or place a few scraps of bread in the bird feeder to attract birds all year round. In the spring, you may even be lucky enough to get a nesting pair of birds in the **tree-top birdhouse**. You can also grow certain shrubs and flowers that encourage butterflies and bees to come into your garden.

For a more structured garden, look at the projects that will help you add an architectural element to the landscape. Building a **garden obelisk**, for example, or maybe two obelisks joined by a shelf, will add geometry to your garden. To add interest at a different level, place a **picket-fence planter** next to it; to add some color, make it with solid sides and paint it. If you already have different levels in your garden, link the levels with **a stepped paved path**. You can put your own personal stamp on your handiwork by adding pebbles or sweet-smelling thyme between the paving slabs.

A garden is more than just a collection of trees, shrubs, and flowers. It can also be a nature reserve for wildlife or a tranquil haven from the daily stresses of modern living. What ever kind of garden you're hoping to create, these twelve garden projects will help you achieve it.

A NOTE ABOUT PLANTS:

The garden projects you choose to make will only look as good as the plants they're with, so make sure you take care of your garden. If you don't know much about plants, invest in a large plant encyclopedia; these list hundreds of plants and the conditions they grow best in, so do some research before you buy—dead plants can be costly. Along with water and food, a little care will turn your planting scheme into the garden of your dreams.

A NOTE ABOUT MEASUREMENTS:

The measurements and quantities given for each project are adaptable for different sizes and areas. Wherever possible, information is given to allow you to calculate how much material you will need to customize the project. When working with tiles, always allow for breakages and buy slightly more than you need. Both imperial and metric measurements are given, but only follow one set of measurements—do not interchange them.

Now that you are ready to attempt your first project, keep the following safety procedures in mind at all times:

❖ Several of the projects suggest protective clothing for certain activities and remember, accidents do happen so it is advisable to wear them;

❖ Always keep powertools unplugged while they are not in use;

❖ If you are working outdoors make sure that any powertool cables are kept clear of water;

❖ When working with a scalpel or utility knife, keep your steadying hand *well away* and *behind* your cutting hand;

❖ Wear goggles when breaking mirror tiles for the water feature (Project 5);

❖ Only cut MDF (Medium Density Fiberboard) in a well-ventilated area and wear the correct type of breathing mask.

HOW THIS BOOK WORKS

A brief introduction describes each project

Tools needed for each project are illustrated

An exploded diagram shows how elements fit together

Detailed photographs provide a visual reference to accompany the text

"Professional Tip" boxes offer expert guidance on achieving the best results

Descriptive text accompanies each photograph, to ensure you know exactly what you are doing

Information boxes provide useful tips on products and procedures, providing alternative options and finishes

Close-up photographs of the finished projects show the end result

Some projects include a variation on the original project

Variations of the projects are also illustrated in detail

GARDEN OBELISK

Add a touch of style to your garden with this wooden obelisk. One can stand alone as a frame for climbing plants or scarlet runner beans. Or make two with shelves running between them for an unusual and attractive way of displaying potted plants.

TOOLS

⅛-inch (3-mm) drill bit

Phillips-head screwdriver bit

Paintbrush

Power drill/ Screwdriver

Tape measure

Pencil

Crosscut saw   Combination square

fence post cap

linking crossbar

vertical support

side unit

MATERIALS

❖ Ten 6-foot (1.8-m) lengths ¾ x 1½-inch (2 x 3.75-cm) pressure-treated wood

❖ No. 6 noncorrosive Phillips-head screws, 1¼ inches (3cm), 1½ inches (3.75cm), and 2 inches (5cm) long

❖ Fence post cap

❖ Wood preservative

VARIATION

To make a second obelisk:

❖ Ten 6-foot (1.8-m) lengths ¾ x 1½-inch (2 x 3.75-cm) pressure-treated wood

❖ No. 6 noncorrosive Phillips-head screws, 1¼ inches (3cm), 1½ inches (3.75cm), and 2 inches (5cm) long

❖ Fence post cap

❖ Wood preservative

For each shelf:

❖ Five 6-foot (1.8-m) lengths, 1⅛ x 1½-inch (2.5 x 3.75-cm) pressure-treated wood

❖ No. 6 noncorrosive Phillips-head screws

NOTE

The wood for this project can be bought from garden centers already pressure-treated with weatherproofer. If it is not treated, remember to weatherproof and, if you wish, stain it before you start work. The wood is sold in packs or as individual lengths.

STARTING OUT - STEPS 1 TO 4

1 The obelisk is made up of two side units in the shape of an inverted V, linked together with crossbars. To make each side unit, take two 6-foot (1.8-m) lengths of wood and lay one on the ground, placing the other directly on top of it. Then, slide the lengths 18 inches (45cm) apart at one end (this will be the foot). Make sure that the top end remains aligned, with one corner of the upper length directly over a corner of the lower length.

2 The top needs to be mitered for a neat fit. To do this, hold the two pieces firmly in position at the top end, making sure that the corners remain aligned and that the foot ends remain 18 inches (45cm) apart. Then, draw a pencil line across the lower length of wood, using the top piece as a guide. Repeat Steps 1 and 2 to mark the miter for the other side unit.

3 Brace each side unit with three crossbars. Measuring from the bottom of one of the lengths of wood, mark the positions of the crossbars at 8, 27¾ and 47¼ inches (20, 70, and 118cm). Use a combination square to draw a line at each of the three marks at right angles to the edge of the wood.

4 Use the marked-up length of wood as a guide to mark the position of the crossbars on the other three lengths of wood. Lay the wood on the ground, so that their ends align. Using your combination square or the edge of a crosscut saw, extend the three pencil lines onto the other three pieces of wood (see below).

PROFESSIONAL TIP

Most crosscut saws today have a square marked where the handle meets the straight edge of the blade. If your combination square is not long enough to reach over four pieces of wood, use the square on the saw. Butt the handle up to the edge of the wood, lining up the straight edge of the saw with the line on the first piece of wood. Then, continue this line over the other pieces of wood with your pencil, using the straight edge of the saw as a guide.

PUTTING IT TOGETHER ~ STEPS 5 TO 8

5 To cut the miters you marked in Step 2, place the marked wood on a workbench. Using a crosscut saw, cut along the line. When sawing along a pencil line, always position your saw on the waste-wood side of the line. Saw steadily to achieve an even cut. Then cut the miter for the other side unit.

6 To screw the top of the side units together, you need to drill pilot holes first. From the pointed top of the mitered piece, measure 3 inches (7.5cm) and 5 inches (12.5cm) down and mark these positions in the center of the wood. Drill a hole at each point using the ⅛-inch (3-mm) drill bit. Do the same to the mitered length of the other side unit.

7 Hold one mitered and one uncut length of wood together, making sure that the top is flat. Place a 1½-inch (3.75-cm) screw in the top pilot hole and screw together, holding the two lengths of wood firmly in position. Then, place a 2-inch (5-cm) screw in the lower pilot hole and screw into place. Repeat for the other side unit.

8 To measure the crossbars, lay one side unit on the ground. Position a 6-foot (1.8-m) length of wood so that its bottom edge is level with the guidelines drawn in Step 4. Mark the outside edges of the side unit on the length of wood in pencil. Move the wood up and along so that the bottom edge aligns with the next guidelines and mark the second crossbar. Then repeat for the third crossbar.

TREATING WOOD

It is essential to protect all the cut ends of the wood with wood preservative. Untreated wood will be affected by moisture, which will cause the wood to rot away, and will also be vulnerable to wood-eating insects. There are a variety of wood preservatives that have color added to them to make a wood stain. These can look attractive because the grain of the wood still shows through. As the plants grow, they will obscure the obelisk, but you will still see glimpses of color amid the foliage.

PUTTING IT TOGETHER - STEPS 9 TO 12

9 Place the wood on a workbench and cut along the marked guides. Measure and cut three more crossbars for the second side unit. You should now have two sets of crossbars, each set with three lengths.

10 The side units are linked by two more sets of crossbars. Each must be 1½ inch (3.75cm) (two widths) longer than the crossbars already cut, to allow for the thickness of the uprights. To cut these, place one crossbar on another length of wood. At either end, place an offcut of wood on its edge and mark this position. Repeat for the other two lengths of crossbar and cut out two sets of crossbars.

11 You should now have four sets of crossbars, two *shorter* sets for the side units and two *longer* sets to link them. Avoid confusion by keeping the sets separated. To attach the shorter crossbars to the side units, drill a pilot hole ¾ inch (2cm) from each end of the shorter crossbars. Position them using the guides drawn earlier and attach each one with 1¼-inch (3-cm) screws.

12 The vertical length (see diagram on page 10) in the center of each side unit provides extra support for climbing plants. Cut four 4-foot (1.2-m) lengths of wood. Turn the side units over, with the crossbars face down. Position a vertical in the center of each side unit. The vertical should protude from the top and bottom crossbar by about 3½ inches (9cm). Screw into place at each crossbar. Repeat for the other side unit.

TAKE CARE

When working on these projects, it is important that you are comfortable and can move around your work area freely and without having to climb over clutter. Make sure the area is tidy and that you have enough room to lay the wood flat. When sawing wood, position and hold it firmly at a comfortable height on a stable object such as a box, stool, workbench or a sawhorse. If you are working outside, make sure that you clear away any garden debris that could trip you as you work.

FINISHING IT OFF – STEPS 13 TO 16

13 Now join the two side units together. On the front of *one* of the side units, drill a pilot hole 1 inch (2.5cm) down from the top. Stand the units up against each other, so that they are facing, their tops are level, and the crossbars are on the outside. Holding the structures together firmly, secure them with a 1½-inch (3.75-cm) screw in the pilot hole.

14 Drill pilot holes ⅜ inch (1cm) from each end of the *longer* (linking) crossbars. Attach only the bottom and middle crossbars to link the two sides, making sure that each end aligns with the crossbars already attached. Screw them into place using 1¼-inch (3-cm) screws.

15 To add the last two vertical supports, drill a pilot hole 3½ inches (9cm) from each end of the supports. Join a vertical to the center of a top crossbar with a 1¼-inch (3-cm) screw. Do the same for the other vertical support. Lay the obelisk with the longer crossbars face down on the ground, and fix the vertical support to the other two crossbars. Turn the obelisk around and attach the last vertical support in the same way.

16 As a finishing touch, add a fence post cap to the top of the obelisk. (If the top is not level and square, lay the obelisk on its side and saw off the top.) Drill a pilot hole in the middle of the post cap. Position the post cap on the top of the obelisk and screw it into position with a 1½-inch (3.75-cm) screw. Finally, paint all the cut ends with wood preservative.

PLANNING YOUR PLANTS

An obelisk allows you to introduce an element of architecture into your garden, so spend some time choosing the best spot. It needs to be in an area where its geometric shape complements the organic shape of the surrounding plants. Remember to check the maximum height of any plants you plan to grow through your obelisk, to make sure that they will not grow too big for the structure. Also, make sure that plants grow evenly around the structure, so that their weight will not cause it to tilt.

VARIATION ~ TWO OBELISKS WITH SHELVES

1 Make more of a feature for your garden by making two obelisks and linking them with one or two slatted shelves. Each obelisk is made in the same way as far as Step 14. In Step 15, do not add a vertical support to the side of the obelisk where the shelves will rest. To make the shelf slats, lay four lengths of wood on the ground, making sure that the ends align. Measure and mark them at 4 feet (1.2m) and cut off these lengths.

2 The shelf slats are supported by three supports, each measuring 8¼ inches (20.5cm), which is the inside measurement of the middle crossbar on the obelisk. On the remaining wood, measure, mark and cut three shelf supports this size. The supports sit at either end of the shelf and across the middle. For a neat finish, cut a miter at each end of the middle support piece.

3 Lay the four 4-foot (1.2-m) lengths down with the ends aligned. To help make the spacing between the shelf slats equal, place three scraps of the ¾-inch (2-cm) wood left over from the obelisk, between the shelf slats. Position a support at one end and screw it in place. Repeat this at the other end, then attach the mitered support piece in the center.

4 The end of the shelf hooks over the middle crossbar of each of the obelisks. You do not need to screw it down, as the weight of the plants will hold it in place. Paint all the cut ends with a wood preservative.

MAKING THE MOST OF YOUR OBELISK

For maximum effect, make two shelves for your obelisk, the second one resting on the bottom horizontal crossbar. Remember that because the obelisk tapers toward the top, the bottom shelf does not need to be as long as the one above. Shelves increase the display area of your basic obelisk. Arrange the plants along the shelf so that their weight is evenly distributed. Avoid placing extremely heavy plants on the shelves, since excessive weight may cause the obelisk to warp or bend unevenly.

A PERFECT WINDOW BOX

A window box overflowing with foliage and flowers adds a dramatic splash of color to even the smallest space. This one is intended to hold plants that have not been removed from their pots, allowing you to change your arrangement at will.

TOOLS

¹/₈-inch (3-mm) drill bit

Putty knife

Paintbrush

Cordless drill/ Screwdriver

Wire cutters

Jigsaw

Pencil

Crosscut saw

Tape measure

Combination square

Hammer

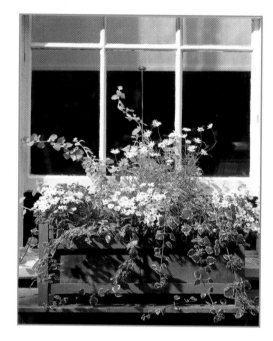

back leg

back

side

base

molding

slate tile

crossbar

NOTE

If you do not have a suitable windowsill on which to position your window box, attach an old shelf unit to the wall under a window. Alternatively, support the box on a row of bricks to aid drainage and place the box at the base of an outside wall.

MATERIALS

❖ One 8-foot (2.4-m) length, or two 4-foot (1.2-m) lengths 1⅛ x 5½-inch (2.5 x 14-cm) pressure-treated wood

❖ Sandpaper

❖ No. 6 noncorrosive Phillips-head screws, 2½ inches (6cm) long

❖ One 1.2-m (4-foot) length 1⅛ x 1½-inch (2.5 x 3.75-cm) pressure-treated wood

❖ One 5-foot (1.5-m) length ¾ x 1½-inch (2 x 3.75-cm) pressure-treated wood

❖ Finishing nails, ⅝ inch (16mm) long

❖ Exterior wood filler

❖ Wood stain or preservative

❖ Roofing slate tiles

❖ Quarter-round molding, ¼ inch (6mm) wide

❖ About four potted plants

VARIATION

❖ Quarter-round molding, ¼ inch (6mm) wide

❖ Finishing nails, ⅝ inch (16mm) long

❖ One 4-foot (1.2-m) length ¾ x 1½-inch (2 x 3.75-cm) pressure-treated wood

❖ Wire mesh, ½-inch (1.25-cm) gauge

❖ Screws

❖ Five ceramic tiles, 6 x 6 inches (15 x 15cm)

❖ Sandpaper

❖ Cedar trellis

STARTING OUT - STEPS 1 TO 4

1 Mark out the basic box: on the length of 5½-inch (14-cm) wide wood, measure and mark the following lengths: 31¾ inches (79cm) for the base, 29½ inches (74cm) for the back, and two lengths of 8½ inches (21.5cm) for each side. Use a combination square to help you draw straight lines across the wood at each of these points.

2 Cut each of the lengths of wood along the lines you have drawn. When you have cut the four pieces, lightly sand the cut ends to remove any splinters. Do not sand the ends too smoothly because they will not be consistent with the overall rough texture of the wood.

3 On one of the side pieces draw a line 1 inch (2.5cm) in from one of the short sides. Within this width, drill a pilot hole in each corner. Do the same for the other side piece. Attach the side pieces to the back piece with a screw in each pilot hole.

4 Drill pilot holes into each corner of the base, about ½ inch (1.25cm) in from the edges. Place the base on top of the back and sides so that the gap (for drainage) is toward the back of the window box. Hold the base firmly and secure it into the side pieces through the pilot holes, using the 2½-inch (6-cm) screws.

PROFESSIONAL TIP

If you make absolutely sure that all the box sides are exactly equal in height and that right angles are accurate, then the box will be easy to assemble. Check the right angles using a combination square. Making square cuts with a hand saw will be easier if you clamp a length of scrap wood along the cutting line to guide the blade. Sand raw edges only lightly to prevent rounding of the angles and for a more secure bond, apply a thin coat of wood glue to the pieces before screwing them together.

PUTTING IT TOGETHER – STEPS 5 TO 8

5 On the piece of 1⅛-by-1½-inch (2.5-by-3.75-cm) wood, measure and mark two 11½-inch (29.5-cm) lengths for the back legs and two 12-inch (30-cm) lengths for the front legs (see below). Cut these lengths out, then lightly sand the cut ends of each leg.

6 The front of the window box is made from two crossbars. Measure and mark two lengths of 28½ inches (71.5cm) on the ¾-by-1½-inch (2-by-3.75-cm) wood and cut these out. Lightly sand the cut ends to remove any splinters.

7 To make the front panel, mark a point 1¾ inches (4.5cm) and 8½ inches (21cm) from one end on the narrow side of each front leg. Draw a straight line across the wood at these points. On the wider side of each leg, mark a point 2½ inches (6cm) and 9¼ inches (23cm) from the same end, and drill pilot holes at these points. Screw the crossbars to the legs, aligning the bottom edge of each crossbar with one of the lines drawn on the narrow side of the legs.

8 On the narrow side of the back legs, mark a line 3 inches (7.5cm) and 9 inches (22.5cm) from one end. Mark and drill two evenly spaced pilot holes in between these two lines, but on the wider face of each leg. Align the pencil marks with the top and bottom of the back of the box, and screw the legs in place. Turn the box over and place the front panel you made in Step 7 on top. Align the pencil marks and secure in place.

PROFESSIONAL TIP

Before you cut the legs, consider the way your windowsill lies. Windowsills usually slope away from the window to allow rainwater to drain off. By making the front legs slightly longer than the back legs, the window box is set at an angle opposite to that of the sill. This allows the base of the box to remain level and ensures that none of the plants become waterlogged—a possibility if the window box tilts at an angle. If your windowsill is completely level, cut all the legs the same length.

PUTTING IT TOGETHER – STEPS 9 TO 12

9 Make an interior frame for the front panel of the window box to keep the slate tiles in place. Mark the length of the inside front of the box on the quarter-round molding by placing one end of it in one corner of the box, then marking where to cut it at the other end.

10 The molding forms the bottom of the interior frame, but there must be room for a slate tile between the molding and the crossbar at the front. On the inside of the front panel, hold a tile against the crossbars, then push the molding against the bottom of the tile. Secure the molding on the bottom crossbar with finishing nails.

11 Now make the top of the interior frame. Measure and mark a length of ¾-by-1½-inch (2-by 3.75-cm) wood against the inside top of the box, as you did with the molding. Cut the wood to size. Hold a tile in place, as before, and secure the wood to the inside of window box with 1½-inch (3.75-cm) screws.

12 Measure and cut two side pieces from the length of ¾-by-1½-inch (2-by-3.75-cm) wood. You can use a tape measure or you can just mark the length as you did with the molding in Step 9. Repeat for the other side. Drill a pilot hole into the center of each side piece and position them on the inside, level with the front of the interior frame and the top of the window box. Fix them into place with 1½-inch (3.75-cm)

STAINS AND PRESERVATIVES

Wood stains soak into the wood, allowing the character and grain of the wood to show through. Because the stain used here is water-based, the brushes can be cleaned easily with water. Some stains have preservatives added to them, which further protects the wood against the elements. Whether you decide to stain your window box or just treat it with wood preservative, make sure that the product you choose does not contain any hazardous chemicals that could harm the plants. Always check the manufacturer's instructions.

FINISHING IT OFF – STEPS 13 TO 16

13 Your window box is almost ready for painting. To give an even surface, fill the visible screw holes with exterior wood filler. Allow the filler to dry (see manufacturer's instructions for drying time).

14 Once the filler is dry, lightly sand over the filled area. You do not need to sand until the filler is completely smooth, just enough so that its texture matches the surrounding wood.

15 Before you paint the window box, protect your work surface with some newspaper and stand the box on top. Using a brush, paint the bottom of the box first, then turn it over and paint the inside. Paint the outside, the front, back, and sides last.

16 Measure and mark two pieces, 6 by 14½ inches (15 by 36.5cm), on the slate. Use chalk to mark this, rather than pencil, since it will show up better. Wearing goggles, hold the slate firmly on the edge of a table or workbench and cut along the lines with a jigsaw. Place the cut slate into the panel at the front of the window box.

CHANGING THE LOOK OF YOUR WINDOW BOX

Ceramic tiles come in a variety of colors, designs, and finishes—and the beauty of this window box is that you can change the tiles whenever you wish. Simply slot your chosen tiles into the interior frame in the front panel of the window box. If you decide from the start to use tiles rather than roof slate-tiles, make the interior frame an appropriate size to accommodate them. You can vary the choice of tiles to suit the season or to complement the plants you have chosen for your window box.

VARIATIONS ~ ALTERNATIVE FRONT PANELS

1 A piece of cedar trelliswork slotted into the interior frame makes an alternative front panel for the window box. Expand the trelliswork and lay it down so that it forms perfect diamond shapes. It may be helpful to clamp a length of wood to the trellis to hold it rigid as you cut it. Measure the inside of the front panel and transfer the measurement to the front of the trellis to fit.

2 Use a long straight edge, such as a length of wood, to mark the trellis. Use a jigsaw to cut along these lines; this will be easier than using a crosscut saw (see below). Lightly sand the cut ends, then stain the trelliswork if you wish. Saturate the cut ends with wood preservative to prevent water penetration. When the stain is dry, position the trelliswork in the frame at the front of the box.

3 Mesh can also be used as a front panel. Measure the length and height of the inside of the frame and transfer these measurements to the mesh—the mesh needs to overlap the inside of the frame. Cut the mesh with wire cutters. With the box face down, place the mesh on the inside. Hold it in place with finishing nails: hit the nail in halfway, then hit it on the side so that it bends over.

4 Cutting miters at the top of the legs makes an attractive finish. Mark the midpoint at the top of each side of the legs. Then, on the edge of each leg, mark a point 1½ inches (3.75cm) down from the top. Join these points to the midpoint at the top. Lay the box on its side and saw along these diagonal lines to cut the miters. Once cut, lightly sand the ends.

PROFESSIONAL TIP

Cedar trelliswork needs to be cut with care to prevent it from falling apart. When measuring and marking the lines to cut make sure they are close to the fixing points on the trelliswork. Even if the trelliswork does collapse, you can fix it into the frame on the window box, which will then support it. To repair a broken trellis, gently hammer in small finishing nails. The pins will not be noticed if you use a nail set to push them into the wood. You can then cover them with exterior wood filler.

ROTUND BIRD FEEDER

Encourage birds to visit your garden by providing them with a place to rest and feed in safety. This simple feeder, with its attractive overlapping slatted roof, can either be suspended from the branch of a tree or stand on top of a pedestal.

TOOLS

Nail set

Pencil

Paintbrush

Utility knife

Power drill/ Screwdriver

Jigsaw

Tape measure

Hammer

Combination square

NOTE

When positioning your bird feeder, make the safety of the birds your prime consideration. Do not stand it on top of any pedestal that can be scaled by cats. Similarly, do not hang it in a tree that is frequented by cats or squirrels. Bird feeders are fun for children, who can make up their own birdseed cakes for birds to enjoy. But having tempted birds to your garden, be prepared to go on feeding them, for they will become dependent on the food you offer.

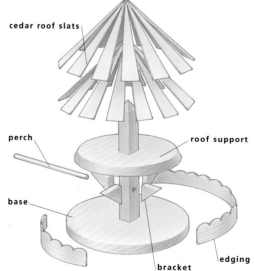

cedar roof slats

perch

base

roof support

bracket

edging

MATERIALS

❖ Pine shelf, 2 by 4 feet (60 by 120cm), ¾ inch (2cm) thick

❖ Piece of scrap wood, at least 16 inches (40 cm) long and a nail (see Step 1)

❖ Pressure-treated wood, 2 by 2 inches (5 by 5cm), 2 feet (60cm) long

❖ Cedar fencing, 4 feet (1.2m) long, ⅜ inch (1cm) thick

❖ Plywood, 18 by 24 inches (45 by 60cm), ⅛ inch (3mm) thick

❖ Small round object to use as a guide

❖ Wood adhesive

❖ Wood stain or varnish

❖ Finishing nails, ¾ inch (2cm) long

❖ No. 8 screws, 1½ inches (3.75cm) and 2 inches (5cm) long

❖ Cardboard (optional, see Step 9)

❖ Oval nails, 2cm (¾ in) long

❖ Drill bit, ⅛ inch (3mm) in diameter

VARIATION

❖ Doweling, ½ inch (1.25cm) in diameter, at least 10 inches (25cm) long

❖ Drill bit, ½ inch (1.25cm) in diameter

❖ Wooden drawer knob

❖ Hook

❖ Chain

STARTING OUT – STEPS 1 TO 4

1 Start by drawing two circles on the pine shelf—one 15 inches (37.5cm) in diameter, the other 16 inches (40cm). To make a "compass" large enough, hammer a small nail through one end of the piece of scrap stock. Mark points 7½ inches (17.5cm) and 8 inches (20cm) from the nail and drill a hole, just big enough for a pencil. Make a small hole in the pine to rest the nail in, then draw the circles using the nail as the pivot.

2 Measure a 17-inch (42.5-cm) length on the pressure-treated wood. (This will be the post in the middle of your bird feeder.) Place the wood over the edge of a table or workbench and cut the length off.

3 Trace around the end of the post in the middle of each circle. To do this accurately, draw a line through the nail hole in the center of each circle. Then draw another line at right angles to this line, also passing through the nail hole at the center. Position the corners of the post on these lines and then draw around the post with a pencil.

4 Place the pine on a table or workbench, and using your jigsaw, cut out the 16-inch (40-cm) circle with a jigsaw. Then, adjust your jigsaw to a 45° angle and cut out the 15-inch (37.5-cm) circle at this angle. The sloped edge will make it easier to attach the roof later.

PROFESSIONAL TIP

Sometimes you need to cut out an area in the middle of a piece of wood without cutting into it from the side (see Step 5). To do this, drill a short row of small holes (on the waste side of the guidelines on the wood) in such a way that the holes join together, to make an opening large enough for you to fit the blade of the jigsaw through. You may need to push a screwdriver or sharp object through the holes to join them together. Once you have inserted the jigsaw blade, you can cut along the guidelines.

PUTTING IT TOGETHER – STEPS 5 TO 8

5 Cut out the squares for the post in the center of each circle (see the tip on page 27). It is better if you undercut the first time because you can trim or sand it to fit in Step 8.

6 To make the point at the top end of the post, mark the midpoint on each of the top edges of the post. Using a combination square, draw a line at 45° from this mark to the long edges of the post on all sides. Cut these portions off and sand the rough edges to remove any splinters.

7 Using the wood left over from the cut circles, make four brackets (see below). Once you have cut these, sand the edges. Drill a pilot hole into each bracket through the width of the longest side. Measure 6¾ inches (17cm) down from the top of the post. Use a combination square to draw a straight line around the post at this point. Set each bracket on this line and attach each one to the post with a 2-inch (5-cm) screw.

8 Push the post through the hole in the larger circle to make the base. It should be a snug fit. Push the post through the smaller circle so it rests on the brackets. Secure this in place through the top of the circle with 1½-inch (3.75-cm) screws. For extra security, hammer some nails through the base at an angle, so that they enter the post.

MAKING BRACKETS

The easiest brackets to make are right-angled triangles. Draw two perpendicular lines 2¼ inches (5.5cm) long. Join them to make the third line of the triangle and cut the triangle out. When joining the brackets to the post, remember that if screws are put directly into wood there is a risk of splitting it. Drilling pilot holes prevents splitting and ensures accuracy. Use a drill bit one size smaller than the screw size and drill to at least half its depth. This will allow the screw threads to fix securely.

PUTTING IT TOGETHER – STEPS 9 TO 12

9 The roof is made up of two different-sized slats made from the plywood; you need twelve of each. One set of slats measure 3 x 12 inches (7.5 x 30cm) and the others measure 2½ x 12 inches (6 x 30cm). Cut out all 24 pieces with a jigsaw. If necessary, make a cardboard template. You will need to make two triangles 12 inches (30cm) high, one with a 2½-inch (6-cm) base, the other with a 3-inch (7.5-cm) base.

10 Take all the 3-inch-(7-cm-) wide slats and hold them together on their sides. Using a pencil or pen, measure 1 inch (2.5cm) from the wide end. Using a combination square, draw a straight line at this point across all the edges. These marks will act as a guide so that you can align the slats when attaching them to the bird feeder. Do the same for the other slats.

11 Start assembling the roof by fixing four of the 3-inch (7.5-cm) slats to the top of the post in the same position as the four points of the compass. Hold each one in place with a finishing nail at the top of each slat. Leave the bottom edge loose for the moment.

12 Now position two 3-inch (7.5-cm) slats in between each of the four already in place. Nail these to the post at the top and trim the points with a utility knife if they overlap at the top. When all twelve slats are in place there should be a gap of about 1½ inches (3.75cm) between each one. When you are happy with their positions, secure them in place at the bottom with finishing nails.

ATTACHING THE SLATS

This type of roof is built up in layers, with the top slats filling the gaps and slightly overlapping the ones below. Any wear and tear on the roof will come from the weather, not from the bird visitors, so the shape of the slats is very important, and you should aim for a snug fit. Finishing nails are sufficient to secure the slats, and they are small enough to tap in place without splitting the wood. To make it easier to fit all the tips of the slats, sand back the mitered edges at the top of the post.

FINISHING IT OFF – STEPS 13 TO 16

13 The slightly smaller slats form the overlaps on the roof. Fix these into place with a finishing nail at the top and bottom. Trim the top of the slats with a utility knife for a neat finish.

14 Cut two lengths of cedar, one 15 inches (37.5cm) long, and the other 30 inches (75cm) long. Draw two parallel lines along the length, one 1¼ inches (4cm) from the bottom, the other 1¾ inches (5cm) from the bottom. Using a round object as a guide, draw curves in between these parallel lines. Cut out the pattern with a jigsaw.

15 Using wood adhesive, glue the scalloped pieces into place around the edge of the base. Tack it securely into place with evenly spaced finishing nails. Leave two gaps of about 2 inches (5cm) between the scalloped pieces to allow rainwater to escape and also to make cleaning the bird feeder easier.

16 Stain or varnish the bird feeder to protect it from the elements. The stain will improve with age and a winter outside will season the bird feeder and make it look even more attractive.

BENDING WOOD

When you have cut out the scalloped edge for the bird feeder, you may find it difficult to bend it into shape. Get someone to hold it in position while you glue and pin the edge around the base. If you experience difficulty when attaching it to the bird feeder, try soaking your scalloped edge in water for about one hour. This should make it more pliable since wood is easier to bend when wet. If you soak the wood, remember that you will have to wait until the wood has dried out a little before you paint it.

VARIATION – A HANGING FEEDER

1 You may like to add a perch to the bird feeder. Measure and cut a piece of doweling to a length of about 10 inches (25cm). This will be a suitable size for most small birds.

2 Drill a hole in the post ½ inch (1.25cm) in diameter and work the dowel through—it needs to be quite a snug fit so that the perch is secure. Make sure it is roughly even on each side, and then paint it with a wood stain or varnish.

3 To attach a hook, you need to fit the top of your bird feeder with a wooden drawer pull first. Cut the bottom off the wooden drawer knob— you will need to secure it in a vise to steady it as you cut. Then hollow it out slightly with a drill so that it will sit on the pointed top of the bird feeder. Using wood adhesive, glue the drawer knob into position and protect it with wood preservative or varnish.

4 Choose a hook that is long enough to go through the drawer knob and into the post. Screw the hook through the middle of the drawer knob. (Depending on the size of your hook, you may have to drill a pilot hole first.) Using a length of chain, hang your bird feeder from the desired location.

WEATHERPROOFING THE CROWN

Any sawn edges of the slats must be saturated with wood stain so that the preservative can sink right into it. The crown will be even more watertight if it is capped and we used part of a wooden drawer knob for ours. This had the advantage of also being strong enough to take a hanging hook. You could substitute a crown of zinc, copper or asphalt material cut to a decorative scallop. But whatever you choose, make sure that you seal all screw or pin holes with exterior wood glue, in order to prevent water from getting in.

PICKET-FENCE PLANTER

Lend an air of decorative distinction to your garden with this spacious planter. The sides can be in "picket-fence" style if you want a rustic effect. Alternatively, use beveled clapboard to make solid sides and paint it a sophisticated black.

TOOLS

⅛-inch (3-mm) drill bit

1-inch (2.5-cm) spade drill bit

Pencil

Combination square

Cordless drill/ Screwdriver

Phillips-head screwdriver bit

Tape measure

Paintbrush

Nail set

Hammer

Crosscut saw

MATERIALS

❖ Eight 6-foot (1.8-m) lengths pressure-treated wood, ¾ x 1½ inches (2 x 3.75cm)

❖ Piece of plywood, 17 x 17 inches (42.5 x 42.5cm), ½ inch (1.25cm) thick

❖ Oval brad nails, 1½ inches (3.75cm) long

❖ Noncorrosive Phillips-head screws, 1¼ inches (3cm) long

❖ Four fence post caps

❖ Wood preservative

❖ Planter, 12 inches (30cm) in diameter

VARIATION

❖ Four 6-foot (1.8-m) lengths plain bevel clapboard, 3½ inches (9cm) wide

❖ Finishing nails, ¾ inch (2cm) long

❖ Wood stain

filler block

post cap

corner bracket

base

crossbar

NOTE

This planter makes a perfect companion to the garden obelisk (page 10). It provides a simple way to vary the height of the architectural elements in your garden.

STARTING OUT – STEPS 1 TO 4

1 Start by making the corners for the planter. The four corner brackets provide the main structural support and each corner is made from two 18-inch (45-cm) pieces of wood. Measure 18 inches (45cm) on one of the lengths of ¾-by-1½-inch (2-by-3.75-cm) treated wood. Mark the position with a pencil, using a combination square to help you draw a straight line.

2 Saw off this length, remembering to position the saw on the waste side of the line. Use this 18-inch (45-cm) length as a template for the remaining pieces; or measure each piece as you go, and cut out eight more 18-inch (45-cm) lengths.

3 The corners of the planter are joined by crossbars at the top and bottom. You need eight crossbars in total—four at 17½ inches (44cm) long and four at 15½ inches (39cm) long. Measure and cut one 17½-inch (44-cm) length and use this length as a template to cut the other three. Repeat the procedure to cut the four 15½-inch (39-cm) crossbars.

4 Now assemble the corner brackets. Lay one 18-inch (45-cm) length on its narrow face. Place another one on top, on its wide face, so that a right angle is formed between the two lengths to make a corner. Secure the pieces of wood together by hammering a finishing nail about 1½ inches (3.75cm) from each end and in the middle. Make the three other corner brackets in the same way.

WORKING SAFELY AND WELL

When sawing wood, make sure that you work at a height that is comfortable for you. If you do not have a workbench or sawhorse, an adjustable stool, such as the one used here, can be altered to suit the individual and is ideal for sawing small lengths of wood. Make sure that you can support the wood as you cut it and that you do not need to stretch or stoop while working. Position the wood so that your cutting line overlaps the edge of your stool and use even strokes when sawing.

PUTTING IT TOGETHER – STEPS 5 TO 8

5 Use a nail set to push the nail heads under the surface of the wood. Hold the nail set firmly on top of the nail and give it one short tap with the hammer. The nail will disappear below the level of the surface. Repeat on all the other nails. This area can then be painted with wood preservative for extra protection.

6 Now mark the positions of the crossbars on each of the corner brackets. Measure and mark points at 3 inches (7.5cm) and 13½ inches (34cm) from one end. Draw lines at these marks with your combination square. Use this corner bracket as a template and transfer the marks to the corresponding positions on the other three corner brackets.

7 Using a ⅛-inch (3-mm) drill bit, drill pilot holes ⅜ inch (1cm) in from each end of the crossbars. Lay two corner brackets parallel to each other so that the guidelines align. Take two of the 17½-inch (44-cm) crossbars and position them so that the top of one goes under the 3-inch (7.5-cm) line, while the bottom of the other goes on top of the 13½-inch (34-cm) line. Screw them in place, then join the other two corner brackets in the same way.

8 Stand these two side sections so that they face each other, making sure that the positions of the crossbars correspond. Lay two of the 15½-inch (39-cm) crossbars on brackets so that they align with the crossbars already in place. Secure the crossbars to the planter with a Phillips-head screw in each pilot hole.

WHAT SIZE PLANTER?

The techniques given here show how to make a square planter. This size is ideal for most small gardens and will comfortably support a plant pot with a 12-inch (30-cm) diameter. You can adjust the size and shape of the planter to suit your garden, but if you make it much larger, you may need to support the base with additional crossbars. Rectangular planters can hold several plant pots or be made to house a plastic window box. Remember not to add too much weight to the planter, or the base may buckle.

PUTTING IT TOGETHER – STEPS 9 TO 12

9 Turn the whole structure upside-down, position the remaining two crossbars in position, and screw them into place. Turn the planter right-side up and you will find that you have a self-supporting structure.

10 To make the base, measure the inside dimensions of the planter. The base should be a 17-inch (42.5-cm) square, but you should always measure your own. Cut out the base if necessary, then use the straight edge of the saw to draw two diagonal lines, from corner to corner, across the base.

11 The planter is designed with picket-fence sides. Each side needs four pickets, with each picket measuring 16¾ inches (42cm). Measure and cut a piece of pressure-treated wood 16¾ inches (42cm) long. To make the pointed peak, mark the midpoint at the top, then mark 1½ inches (3.75cm) down either side. Draw two diagonal lines between these marks and the midpoint, then saw off the two corners.

12 Use this picket as a template to cut the other 15 pickets. Lay the picket on a length of wood and trace around the point and the end. Once drawn, cut this picket out and repeat for the remaining pickets.

CHOOSING YOUR SAW

There are a variety of saws available from most hardware stores. A crosscut saw, or handsaw as it is sometimes called, is a versatile and useful cutting tool for both wood and synthetic boards. It usually has a blade up to about 26 inches (65cm) long and a wooden or plastic handle. It is particularly useful for rough cutting. The teeth of the saw also come in different sizes—the smaller and more closely spaced the teeth, the finer the cut. When sawing, always remember to use regular strokes.

FINISHING IT OFF – STEPS 13 TO 16

13 Lay four of the pickets on the ground and place the planter on top of the pickets. Make sure that the points and ends of the pickets align. Using a piece of wood as a guide, space the pickets evenly between the corner brackets. Mark the position of the pickets on the crossbars, and then mark the position of pilot holes on both crossbars within the lines you have just drawn.

14 Drill pilot holes on the crossbars using the ⅛-inch (3-mm) drill bit, then reposition the pickets underneath, using the marks you made as a guide. Again, make sure that the points and the ends of the pickets align. Attach the pickets to the crossbars with a screw in each pilot hole. Then turn the planter onto another side and repeat until the four sides are complete.

15 Place the base in the planter with the lines uppermost. You need to cut out drainage holes for excess water. Mark five holes, one in the center and the others at four corners of a square around it, on the diagonal lines you drew in Step 10. Raise the planter on blocks of scrap lumber to keep the drill from hitting the ground. Cut the holes using the 1-inch (2.5-cm) spade drill bit.

16 Before you add a fence post cap to each corner of the planter, cut a small piece of wood to use as a "filler" block in each corner, to help hold the caps securely. Each filler block should be flush with the top of the corner and sit on top of the crossbar. Nail the filler block in place, then nail a fence post cap on top. Set the nail heads below the surface of the wood and paint all the cut ends and nails with wood preservative.

LOOKING AFTER YOUR PLANTS

Your hard work is done, and now you need to position your planter and add suitable potted plants. Remember to add drainage material at the bottom of the pot and then a soil mixture suitable to the type of plants you plan to grow. Slow-release plant-food granules keep container plants healthy and can be mixed into the soil before planting. Follow the manufacturer's instructions carefully, since overfeeding will burn the plant roots. Remember to water the plants regularly too, as potted plants do tend to dry out quickly.

VARIATION - A PLANTER WITH SOLID SIDES

1 Follow the instructions to make the planter up to and including Step 10. Add the filler blocks following the instructions in Step 16 (see page 38), attaching them to the top of each corner above the horizontal crossbar. Then nail a fence post cap over each corner.

2 To make one side, cut four 17-inch (42.5-cm) lengths of clapboard. Lay the planter on its side and position a piece of clapboard so that its thin edge butts the top crossbar of the planter. Secure in place with finishing nails on either side. Nail the next piece so that the thin edge overlaps the thick edge of the one already in place. Position and nail the other two pieces in the same way.

3 Turn the planter upside down and repeat the process on the opposite side with four more 17-inch (42.5-cm) lengths. Then, cut eight 16-inch (40-cm) lengths of featheredge for the other two sides. Attach these to the sides of the planter as before.

4 Taking care not to splash the surrounding area, paint the planter inside and out with a water-base wood stain. While you wait for the paint to dry, measure and add a base as in Step 15 (see page 38), remembering to drill drainage holes. Then position the planter in the garden and add a pot of your favorite plants.

PROFESSIONAL TIP

Use a water-base wood stain for this planter. It is nontoxic to plants or animals and any spills or splashes can be removed quite easily with a damp cloth. As with any wooden structure, the look of this planter will improve with age.

After a season or two of exposure to the elements, the planter will have weathered and will take on a more rustic look. The type of pot you use inside this solid-sided planter is a matter of practicality rather than aesthetics, since it will not be visible.

WATER FEATURE

Water features make a welcome and attractive addition to any garden. The advantage of this one is that it can go anywhere, does not need a lot of space, and requires no electricity or plumbing. It is also inexpensive and simple to make!

TOOLS

Putty knife

Scissors

Bucket or bowl

Trowel

Gardening gloves

Dressmaker's tape measure

Tile cutter

Tenon saw

Pencil

Carpenter's level

NOTES

Choose a sunny spot in your garden for this feature because waterlilies do not like shade.

Mirror tiles alternating with blue ceramic strip tiles maximize the reflection from the water. Remember to buy a few extra mirror tiles in case they break when you are cutting them.

Use gloves when working with cement, especially if you have sensitive skin.

burlap

lily basket

ceramic tiles

mirror tiles

glazed pot

MATERIALS

❖ Glazed plant pot; the one used here is 20 inches (50cm) high and 25 inches (65cm) in diameter

❖ Two-part epoxy putty

❖ Piece of scrap wood, at least 6 inches (15cm) long

❖ Ready-mixed quick-drying waterproof cement and a stick for stirring

❖ Mirror tiles (see Step 1 to calculate number)

❖ Ceramic strip tiles, (see Step 1 to calculate number)

❖ All-purpose waterproof wall tile adhesive and grout

❖ Dwarf lily, such as *Nymphaea pygmaea* 'Alba', double marsh marigold, and iris

❖ Lily basket

❖ Piece of burlap sheet, at least 18 x 18 inches (45 x 45cm)

❖ Aquatic compost

❖ Gravel

❖ Several bricks (see Step 16)

❖ Stick with rounded end

❖ Sponge

❖ Sandpaper

PUTTING IT TOGETHER – STEPS 1 TO 4

1 To work out how many tiles you need, measure the inside circumference of the pot with a dressmaker's tape measure. The width of one ceramic strip tile and one mirror tile together is 2 inches (5cm) so divide the circumference by 2 inches (5cm) to work out how many mirror and strip tiles you will need. (You can cut the mirror tiles to a different width in Step 6, but you will have to work out how many you need.)

2 Knead together the two-part epoxy putty following the manufacturer's instructions. Once it is a uniform color, push it firmly into the drainage holes at the bottom of the pot, making sure that they are filled completely. This will stop the water from leaking out when the pot is full. Leave the putty to dry.

3 To create a level surface for the tiles, you will need to fill the slight depression under the rim on the inside of the pot with cement. To make a level for the cement, cut the scrap piece of wood to the same length as the tiles, 6 inches (15cm), using a tenon saw.

4 Wearing a pair of gloves, pour the cement into a bowl. Make a well in the middle, then slowly add some water. Use a stick to mix the cement to a thick consistency, adding more water or cement as necessary. If you have not mixed enough to coat the rim of the pot, don't worry—just mix some more to the same consistency as you go.

PROFESSIONAL TIP

When mixing cement, remember that it sets very quickly, so always mix small quantities. Take care not to add too much water or the cement will be sloppy and difficult to work with. As a general rule, the cement is the right consistency when a stick or twig will stand vertically in the mix. If your cement is too dry, it will crumble and won't hold properly. In this case, simply add more water, a little at a time, until the cement is the required consistency.

PUTTING IT TOGETHER – STEPS 5 TO 8

5 Using a putty knife, apply a coat of cement to the inside of the pot, extending down 6 inches (15cm). Take the cut piece of wood and hold it at right angles to, and level with, the top of the pot (use a carpenter's level to help you). Press down firmly, then slowly bring the wood around the pot towards you, pushing any excess cement away. Fill in any gaps with cement, then go over them again with the wood.

6 Now prepare the mirror tiles. Set the gauge on the tile cutter to a width of 1½ inches (3.75cm). Butt the mirror tile up against the gauge, and bring the handle toward you to score the surface of the tile. Remember, always wear gloves and goggles when cutting mirror tiles.

7 Now bring the scored mirror tile up to the cutter, and position it under the cutting bars. Make sure that you hold the tile straight on the horizontal and bring the handle down in one swift movement. The required width will snap off. You should now have a mirror tile measuring 1½ x 6 inches (3.75 x 15cm). Repeat for the other mirror tiles.

8 Sand all the edges of the mirror tiles to prevent accidents to people, pets or wildlife. To do this safely, lay a sheet of sandpaper on a flat surface and hold the mirror tile face down, at 45° to the sandpaper. Rub the tile back and forth several times to blunt the edges.

GEOMETRIC TILING

If you are feeling adventurous, or are an experienced tiler, you may like to try creating a more intricate design with the tiles. You can buy mosaic tiles either loose or in sheets, which can be cut to size. They come in a range of colors and can be mixed with the mirror tiles if you wish. You need to make a paper pattern the same size as the inside of the pot and lay out the pieces on it. Allow enough space between the tiles for the cement and transfer the pattern onto the pot, working a small section at a time.

PUTTING IT TOGETHER – STEPS 9 TO 12

9 When the cement is dry (about two hours), apply an even coat of tile adhesive using the applicator supplied with the adhesive. The glue should cover the surface of the cement strip all the way around the inside of the pot. The notches in the applicator create a good surface for the tiles, enhancing the bond.

10 Start fixing the tiles in place. You will need to use a carpenter's level to make sure that the tiles remain vertical. Start with a mirror tile and hold it in place with the carpenter's level on top. Adjust the position of the tile as necessary so that it is vertical before you push it firmly into place.

11 Alternate ceramic and mirror tiles, keeping them at right angles to the top of the pot. As you push the tiles into place, excess adhesive will squeeze out of the gaps between them. Wipe this away with a sponge or cloth before it dries. Remember to keep checking that the tiles are vertical, using the carpenter's level to help you.

12 When the adhesive is dry (it should take about two hours), grout the tiles to prevent water from getting behind them. Use the straight edge of the adhesive applicator to apply the grout over the joints and in a layer around the top and bottom of the tiles. Run a stick in between the gaps of the tiles to compact the grout. Wipe off any excess grout on the tiles with a wet sponge before it dries.

PROFESSIONAL TIP

When choosing the tile adhesive, make sure that you select a waterproof variety since it will be under water when it is dry. You may find that you need to choose between a thin-bed and a thick-bed adhesive. Thin-bed adhesive is simpler to use and can easily be spread to the required thickness – about ⅛ inch (3mm). Thick-bed adhesive is more difficult to work with and is not recommended for beginners. It is used on uneven surfaces and requires considerable tiling skill.

FINISHING IT OFF – STEPS 13 TO 16

13 While you are waiting for the grout to dry, prepare the lily for planting. Line the lily basket with burlap, allowing the excess to hang over the sides. The burlap allows the plant's roots to grow through it and holds the compost in place. With a trowel, fill the basket with about 2 inches (5cm) of aquatic compost.

14 Place a dwarf lily, (*Nymphaea pygmaea*) carefully in the basket on top of the compost so that the top of the root ball is about 1½ inches (3.75cm) below the top of the basket. Add compost around the plant, but do not put any on the top of the root ball, which should protrude about 1 inch (2.5cm) above the soil.

15 You need to cover the top of the compost with gravel to hold it in place and prevent it from floating to the surface when you add the water. Slowly and gently tip the gravel on top of the compost, leveling it out with your hands. You do not need much gravel, just enough to cover the surface. Trim any excess burlap from the sides of the basket with scissors.

16 Use a scrap piece of burlap to polish the tiles and give them a real shine. Then put a 4-inch (10-cm) layer of gravel on the bottom of the pot. Carefully position the lily basket on this or, if necessary, add height with a few bricks so that the lily floats on the water surface. You can add other plants, such as a double marsh marigold and an iris, which would need brick supports to raise them to the correct height.

FILLING YOUR WATER FEATURE

Decide where you want to position your water feature and move it into place before you fill it with water because it will be heavy and difficult to move once it is full. When filling the pot, put the hose at the bottom and turn the tap on gently so as not to disturb the compost and gravel in the plants too much. When filling or cleaning the water feature, allow the water to overflow from the top of the pot. This will flush through any debris and prevent the water from becoming stagnant.

A HOMEMADE HAMMOCK

What could be more idyllic than relaxing in a hammock on a hot summer afternoon with a good book and a long, cool drink? With this hammock, you can enjoy all this and feel virtuous, as you have done all the hard work!

TOOLS

¼-inch (6-mm) drill bit

Countersink bit

Scissors

Tape measure

Power drill/Screwdriver

Pencil

Hammer

Tenon saw

metal ring

crosspiece

heavy duty canvas

doweling

nylon rope

MATERIALS

❖ Heavy-duty canvas 36 x 80 inches (90 x 200cm)

❖ Double-sided carpet tape, 2 inches (5cm) wide

❖ Doweling, ½ inch (1.25cm) in diameter, 5 feet (1.5m) long

❖ Doweling, 1 inch (2.5cm) in diameter, 6 feet (1.8m) long

❖ ⅜-inch (1-cm) brass eyelets, including the tap and die

❖ Nylon rope, ³⁄₁₆ inch (½cm) thick, 63 feet (20m) long

❖ Two metal rings, 2 inches (5cm) in diameter

❖ Two metal cleats

❖ Sandpaper

❖ Framing square (optional, see Step 2)

NOTES

Most arts and crafts shops or major department stores sell canvas. Buy the heaviest weight available. If you prefer, you can use deckchair canvas, which will provide a dramatic splash of color.

The nylon cord used for this project has a breaking strain of 200 pounds (90kg) and all materials suggested here are of the best quality. However, we do not recommend that the hammock be used by more than one person of average weight at any one time.

STARTING OUT - STEPS 1 TO 4

1 If your canvas is not cut to size, spread it out on a flat surface and mark a rectangle measuring 36 x 80 inches (90 x 200cm). Use a straight length of wood or a long ruler to draw the lines. Cut along the lines with a pair of scissors.

2 Draw a line parallel to, and 2 inches (5cm) from, each edge of the canvas. Then draw a line 4 inches (10cm) in from each side. These guidelines show you where to stick the double-sided carpet tape. Make sure that all the corners are squared up—you may need to use a framing square to help you.

3 Starting at one end of the hammock, firmly stick the double-sided tape to the canvas between the two lines you have just drawn. The guidelines will help you keep the double-sided tape straight. When pressing the tape to the canvas, take care that it does not crease or buckle.

4 Measure and cut out two lengths of 28 inches (70cm) on the ½-inch (1.25-cm) diameter doweling. Keeping the canvas and tape as flat as possible, carefully peel off the backing paper on the double-sided tape on the two short sides. Double-sided tape is very sticky and you may need someone to help you keep the canvas flat.

SIZING YOUR HAMMOCK

You can make a hammock any size you wish. The size given here is for an average height. If you are below average height, or if you are making the hammock for a child, you can make the hammock shorter. A short person on a long hammock means that it will sink lower than usual in the middle. To make a hammock that is an appropriate length for your personal use, add 90cm (3 ft) to your own height – this figure will be the length of canvas you need to buy. Then follow the rest of the steps to make the hammock.

PUTTING IT TOGETHER – STEPS 5 TO 8

5 Rub the ends of the doweling that you already cut in Step 4 with sandpaper to eliminate any splinters. On the short side of the canvas, position one of the dowels on the tape against its outside edge, and press it down firmly.

6 Fold the canvas over the dowel so that the edge of the canvas aligns with the far edge of the tape and the guidelines you drew earlier. Press the canvas down firmly onto the tape, taking care not to crease or buckle it. Repeat Steps 5 and 6 for the other short side of the canvas.

7 To avoid bulky corners when you fold the canvas over, cut out a small square, measuring about 2 inches (5cm), from the corners of the hammock.

8 Now peel off the backing strip on one of the long sides and fold the canvas over so that the canvas edge aligns with the guideline drawn in Step 2. Work your way slowly down the side of the canvas, pressing the tape firmly in place. Repeat for the other long side.

CARPET TAPE

Carpet tape is essentially a very strong double-sided tape and is used here in place of a sewn hem. (A sewn hem on a thick canvas would require an industrial sewing machine!) The advantage is that the fabric is bonded into a double thickness, preventing fraying at the edges, and making a stronger bed to fix eyelets into. The tape itself does not support the weight, but because it is originally intended to hold carpet down, it can be relied upon to last as long as the canvas does (see Notes on page 48).

PUTTING IT TOGETHER – STEPS 9 TO 12

9 At each short end of the hammock, mark the center points of the seven eyelets. Place a tape measure across the end inside the ridge made by the covered dowel and make a mark at 1, 6, 11, 16, 21, 26, and 31 inches (2.5, 15, 27.5, 40, 52.5, 65, and 77.5cm) from one end. Mark these same measurements at the other short end.

10 Place the canvas on a hard surface, such as a small paving slab. Using the tap and die provided in the eyelet kit, place the die directly under the first pencil mark. Push the tap onto the canvas so that it fits snugly into the die underneath. Hit the tap sharply with a hammer, cutting a neat circle in the canvas.

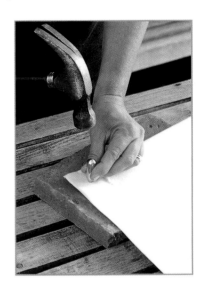

11 Cut all the remaining holes in the same way, then put in the eyelets. The eyelets come in two parts. Place the part with the flange in the die and push this up through the hole in the canvas. Put the other part of the eyelet over the flange and hold it in place with the tap. Hit the tap sharply with a hammer to join the two parts together. Repeat for the other eyelets.

12 There are also decorative eyelets in the long sides of the hammock. Mark their positions 1 inch (2.5cm) from the edge of the folded canvas. From one end, measure and mark the center points of the holes at 8, 10, 17, 19, 26, 28, 35, 37, 44, 46, 53, 55, 62, and 64 inches (20, 25, 42.5, 47.5, 65, 70, 87.5, 92.5, 110, 115, 132.5, 137.5, 155, and 160cm). Make holes at these points as before and then insert the eyelets.

ALL ABOUT EYELETS

Eyelets are obtainable from marine (boat) suppliers and are used to strengthen holes in canvas sails and nylon tarpaulins. They are sold complete with assembly tools and instructions and come in a range of sizes. Most eyelets are brass, but plastic versions are also on the market. They seal the raw edges of the fabric and spread the strain, which is their function on the shorter ends of the hammock. However, besides being practical, they also look very decorative, and they are used in this way on the long edges.

PUTTING IT TOGETHER – STEPS 13 TO 16

13 To make the crosspieces, measure and mark two 32-inch (80-cm) lengths of 1-inch (2.5-cm) diameter doweling. Support the doweling so that the waste wood overhangs the edge of your workbench, and cut out the lengths.

14 Smooth the sawn edge with a piece of sandpaper. Then, using a long ruler or a straight piece of wood as a guide, draw a line along the length of each dowel.

15 Make a mark ⅞ inch (2cm) in from one end and then mark every 2¾ inches (7cm) along the line (you should have a total of 12 marks along the line). Make sure that the dowel is positioned firmly, then drill holes at each of these points using a ¼-inch (6-mm) drill bit.

16 Do the same for the second piece of doweling. Then countersink each hole on both dowels. Sand each piece smooth with sandpaper.

SAFETY TIPS FOR DRILLING HOLES IN DOWELING

When drilling holes in doweling or any circular piece of wood, take extra care that the wood doesn't slip. Use a vise or c-clamp to hold the wood securely – if the drill slips, your doweling will be ruined. However, if you are an experienced woodworker and are fairly confident using a power drill, you can wedge the doweling into the gaps on a workbench or table, as shown above. But always use an awl or nail to break the surface of the wood before you start drilling. Begin slowly, then speed up.

PUTTING IT TOGETHER – STEPS 17 TO 20

17 You are now ready to start threading the rope through the hammock. The easiest way to do this is to place one end of the hammock near to, and parallel with, the edge of the work table. Hold it in place by hammering a nail through the first eyelet on either side. Measure the midpoint and position the bottom of one of the metal rings 12 inches (30cm) up from this point. Hold the ring in place with a nail.

18 For each end, you will need 24 feet (7.2m) of rope. Wind some adhesive tape around the ends of the rope to make it easier to thread. Thread most of the rope through the ring, leaving about 12 inches (30cm) outside the ring. Thread the rope through the second hole in the dowel and the second eyelet. Thread the rope through the third hole in the dowel, and back through the ring, leaving about 12 inches (30cm) slack.

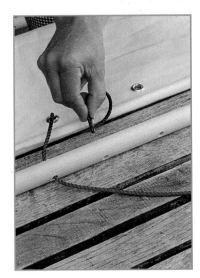

19 Continue threading the rope in this way, leaving the last hole in the hammock and dowel free. Check that the tension of the rope is even in each length, then return the taped end of rope through the ring. Take the other end and double it over to form a loop (see also the diagram on page 110).

20 Hold the loop and the slack lengths of rope and start winding, or whipping, the untaped length of rope around this loop. Pull the rope tight each time. You need to whip it around the loop at least ten times.

PROFESSIONAL TIP

When binding the end of the nylon cord with insulating tape, add an extra twist to make a pointed end which will make threading a whole lot easier. It is important to keep all the lengths evenly matched; this will stop the hammock from twisting and ensure that the weight is evenly distributed along the length of the canvas. Whipping needs practice: try out your technique before working on the hammock. When the tension is right, the effect is very neat and the you will be able to easily pull the loose end up inside the coil.

PUTTING IT TOGETHER - STEPS 21 TO 24

21 After you have whipped the rope, thread it through the back of the remaining loop, while keeping the other length taut. Pull on the rope so that the loop closes around the taped length of rope to form a knot.

22 Holding the whipping firmly, pull the untaped length of rope so that the knot is pulled halfway inside the whipping. Cut both ends of the rope as close as possible to the whipping. Repeat Steps 17–22 for the other end.

23 Cut two 90-inch (2.25-m) lengths of rope for the sides. Wrap tape around the ends as before, and thread the rope through the last hole in the dowel. Pull it through and tie a knot at the untaped end. Weave the rope in and out of the eyelets until you reach the dowel at the other end. Thread the rope through the dowel and secure with a knot. Cut off any excess rope.

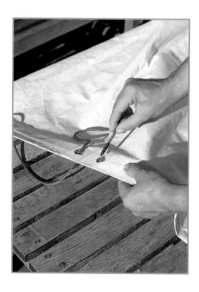

24 Thread the rope along the other side in the same way, knotting the end of the rope after threading it through the dowel. Finally, attach a cleat to each of the rings. Your hammock is now ready for hanging from secure fixings (see below).

WHERE TO HANG YOUR HAMMOCK

The wonderful relaxation of lying in a hammock comes from being suspended and in motion—rocking gently from side to side. The height from the ground is immaterial, but to be on the safe side, we suggest lower rather than higher, especially if young children are likely to clamber into the hammock. Supports obviously need to be sturdy. Choose two strong tree trunks, if you are fortunate enough to have two suitably spaced ones in your garden, or a wall bracket and a tree, or a free-standing hammock support.

A STEPPED PAVED PATH

An informal stepped path makes a charming link between the upper and lower levels of this garden. The emphasis is on the natural look, with rounded beach pebbles and chestnut stakes setting off simulated terra-cotta concrete slabs.

TOOLS

Sledgehammer   Shovel

Brush

Garden spade

Float

Garden sieve

Saw

Rubber mallet

Bucket

Club hammer

Bricklaying trowel

Brick chisel

Garden trowel

Carpenter's level

wooden stakes

bricks

pebbles

paving slabs

MATERIALS

To make two steps, each one measuring 36 x 43 inches (90 x 107.5cm):

❖ Forty wooden stakes, 20 inches (50cm) long

❖ Twenty concrete paving slabs, about 9½ x 9½ inches (24 x 24cm)

❖ Beach pebbles, about 11 pounds (5kg)

❖ Length of wood, the width of the path or longer (see Step 2)

❖ One bucketful garden soil (see Step 3)

❖ One 50-pound (22-kg) bag of gravel (coarse aggregate)

❖ One 50-pound (22-kg) bag each of type 1A Portland cement and masonry cement

❖ Two 50-pound (22-kg) bag of clean, dry, finely-grained building sand

❖ Dishwashing detergent

❖ 14 bricks

❖ Thyme seeds

VARIATION

❖ Sand

❖ Small potted plants, such as herbs

❖ Old paving slabs

NOTE

Two steps are made in this project, which can easily be done in a day. If you want to make a longer run of steps, you must allow a correspondingly longer amount of time in which to complete the work.

56

STARTING OUT - STEPS 1 TO 4

1 Clear the pathway of the old paving as well as any large stones or plants. Next, line both edges of the path with wooden stakes. Push the pointed end of the stake into the ground and hammer it down halfway with a sledgehammer. Hammer the next stake flush against the first, and continue adjusting the depth until the tops make a gentle curve running down the slope of your pathway.

2 To determine the exact width of the path (three slabs wide in this case), lay the concrete slabs on a flat, hard surface, then place some beach pebbles on either side and measure this width. Cut a piece of wood to this width. Hammer in a parallel row of stakes using the wood to measure the distance between the two lines of stakes. Each time you hammer in another stake, use this measure to check its position.

3 You will need to dig foundations for the front of each step to give them extra support. Using your garden spade, mark a line in the soil between the stakes, 36 inches (90cm) from the top of the slope. Dig a trench along this line, the width and depth of the spade. Save a bucketful of the soil you remove to use later and distribute the rest in a suitable part of the garden.

4 Next, mix some concrete. On a hard surface make a mound of 8 shovelfuls of gravel and 3½ shovelfuls of sand. Sprinkle 2 shovelfuls of type 1A Portland cement on top. Mix the three together by pushing your shovel into the mound and lifting and turning the gravel, sand, and cement mixture over. Continue mixing until it is a uniform color throughout.

WOODEN STAKES

Wooden stakes were chosen to act as a natural barrier alongside the path in order to make a gentle, visually pleasing transition between the hard surface of the path itself and the flower beds running alongside it. The stakes have a dual role, being both functional and decorative. Not only do they provide a strong and effective barrier to keep the soil off the path, but with the passage of time and exposure to the weather, they will mellow and look even better as nearby foliage drifts over them.

PUTTING IT TOGETHER – STEPS 5 TO 8

5 Make a cavity in the center of the mound and half fill it with water. (Don't add too much, you need to make a fairly stiff consistency.) Work your way around the mound, pushing the mix into the water. Continue until you have a stiff mix.

6 Scoop the concrete into a bucket with your shovel and pour it into the trench you dug in Step 3. Because it is a stiff mixture, you will need to shake the bucket to help it come out. The concrete should cover the bottom of the trench evenly and be level with the top of the downward slope. Using a float, smooth the surface of the concrete. You may need to add more concrete to the trench to level it off.

7 Then, make some mortar by mixing three parts of clean, dry building sand with one part masonry cement (see below). Use a bricklaying trowel to lay a bed of mortar on top of the concrete.

8 Lay the short edge, or header, of the first brick close to the wooden stakes. Put some mortar on the short edge of the second brick and lay this next to the first, pushing the two together. Lay the next brick in the same way. If you need to cut a brick in half, position a brick chisel about halfway along the top of the brick and hit the chisel with a club hammer. Repeat this on the other sides until the brick breaks.

PROFESSIONAL TIP

Add a squirt of dishwashing liquid to the water before mixing your mortar. The detergent softens the water and makes it easier to work with. In addition to this, it also helps make the mortar more plastic and keeps it from "going off" or hardening too quickly, which sometimes can result in cracking. It is useful to have a mortar that remains workable for a longer period because it allows you time to work at a slower pace, and this is likely to give a neater result.

PUTTING IT TOGETHER - STEPS 9 TO 12

9 Lay a bed of mortar on top of the first row, or course, of bricks. Position the first brick of the second course so that it straddles the joint between two bricks below. Continue laying the second course. Use the trowel to gently tap the bricks down into position each time.

10 Now make sure that the soil of the first step is level. Push the tip of the spade into the soil and drag it gently backward and forward, smoothing the surface so that it is slightly below the top of the bricks. You may need to add or remove soil to achieve a flat surface.

11 Next, mix additional mortar using three parts sand and one part masonry cement. Add water to the mix so it just falls off the trowel. Scoop the mortar into a bucket and pour it over the leveled-out soil. Using the tops of the bricks as your guide, push the mixture around the step with the float to create an even bed of mortar about 1 inch (2.5cm) deep.

12 To make sure water can drain away, the mortar needs to slope down slightly from the top of the step. Take a carpenter's level and place one end on the bricks and the other on the mortar toward the back of the step. The mortar should be slightly higher at the back. Add or remove mortar to achieve this.

PROFESSIONAL TIP

Use a stiff mixture of concrete when laying the foundations, as this will allow you to lay the bricks directly on top, enabling you to complete the project in a day. Don't forget, though, that the mortar and concrete will need time to set. Do not walk on your completed path for at least 24 hours, otherwise you could misalign the slabs and have a uneven path. You may like to add an individual touch such as the date or your initials, which can be done quite simply by pressing pebbles into the wet concrete.

PUTTING IT TOGETHER - STEPS 13 TO 16

13 Temporarily position the paving slabs by laying them lightly on the bed of mortar. Make sure that the first row overlaps the bricks by 2 inches (5cm), and that they are spaced evenly. Using the first row as a guide, position the next row of slabs so that each slab is behind a joint in the first row. Continue until you have positioned all the slabs.

14 When you are happy with their positions, carefully lift each slab off the mortar. You will find that the slabs leave an indentation in the mortar and you can use this as your positioning guide.

15 Place some mortar for the first slab on the step, making sure it covers the top of the brick course. Position the first slab firmly on top of its indentation in the mortar, remembering that it needs to overhang the bricks. Then, take a rubber mallet and gently tap the surface of the slab so that it is secure in the mortar. Put down more mortar and lay the rest of the row in the same way.

16 As you lay the second row of slabs, make sure that you keep a slight downward slope. Lay your carpenter's level on the slabs and use the rubber mallet to tap down the slabs where necessary, to maintain this slope. Continue laying the slabs for the next two rows and check the slope of each row with the level.

PROFESSIONAL TIP

It is vital that both the slabs and the bricks have an equal resistance to frosty conditions. If one crumbles, it will spoil the whole appearance of the path. Before you buy them, make sure you check that the bricks and slabs are suitable for outdoor use and all weather conditions. Modern concrete slabs are cast in faithful reproductions of all manner of natural stones. The molding and tinting is so convincing that it is hard to tell the difference from the real thing.

PUTTING IT TOGETHER – STEPS 17 TO 20

17 Now that the slabs are in place, the areas at the side of each row and the end can be filled with beach pebbles. Take a handful of pebbles and drop them into the mortar. Push them gently into place. As the mortar sets, it will hold the pebbles securely.

18 Being careful not to tread on the first step, make the second step in the same way, following Steps 8 to 17. Remember to use your carpenter's level to check that this step also slopes slightly to allow water to drain away.

19 By the time you have completed the two steps, the mortar in the brickwork will have had a chance to dry. You can now remove any excess from the joints. Take a stick, and, being careful not to gouge too deeply, gently drag it along the horizontal joint, leaving about ½ inch (1.25cm) at each end. Repeat for the other joints. Then, fill in any gaps where the slabs overlap the bricks.

20 Now prepare the bucketful of soil you saved in Step 3. Remove all the stones and break up any big lumps of soil by passing it through a garden sieve.

GIVING A PATH AN IDENTITY

This path is laid without the need to cut any of the paving slabs to size. And the variation of this project (see page 64) uses old broken paving stones. Irregular shapes that arise during the laying can be filled with beach pebbles, which not only look attractive but also help water drain off the steps. Don't worry about trying to match the arrangement of paving slabs between steps. The eccentric nature of the arrangement of the slabs on each step gives the path an individual identity and adds to its rustic charm.

FINISHING IT OFF – STEPS 21 TO 24

21 Using the garden trowel as your measure, mix together eight scoops of soil and four scoops of sand (see below).

22 Spread out this mixture with your trowel, and sprinkle some thyme seeds evenly over the top. Use the trowel to mix the seeds and the soil together.

23 Next, sprinkle the soil mixture over the joints of the slabs with the trowel. Use a brush to push the mixture into the joints between the slabs. Tap it down with the brush making sure that it is tightly compacted into each joint.

24 When all the joints have been filled, brush the mixture onto the next step. With the brush, push the soil mixture into the joints as before. When you have filled all the joints, sweep the remaining soil away. Take care not to get any of the soil around the beach pebbles.

A SWEET-SMELLING PATHWAY

Sieved soil and sand are mixed at a ratio of two to one—two measures of soil to one of sand. This improves the drainage properties of the soil and prevents it from becoming a solid lump in the rain. Thyme seeds are added to this mixture, which is then used to fill the gaps between the slabs. The advantage of the low-growing thyme plant is that it not only breaks up the shapes of the slabs, but as the thyme grows, it will release its subtle perfume, creating an attractive and fragrant pathway.

VARIATION - USING BROKEN SLABS

1 For a different look, you may want to reuse old or chipped paving slabs for your path. Lay down an even thickness of sand, packing it down tightly. Position the irregular-shaped slabs along the length of the path. Use the carpenter's level and a rubber mallet to make sure they are level. In between these slabs, place bricks on their sides, banging them into position, level with the surrounding slabs.

2 Fill other gaps in the path with smaller slabs. Line both sides of the path with beach pebbles, pushing them down hard into the bed of sand.

3 Mix together some sand, soil, and thyme seeds as in Steps 21 and 22 on page 62. Brush this mixture into the gaps between the slabs and bricks. Use the brush to tap the mixture down into the gaps.

4 Small plants, such as potted herbs, provide a useful and attractive finishing touch. Plant these in the larger gaps, near to the sides of the path.

FINDING INSPIRATION

Keep your eyes peeled for unusual or attractive paths when browsing through gardening or style magazines, visiting gardens, or looking at gardening books. Make notes and sketches, or take photographs. These sources will help you come up with something really individual when you create your own path. Be on the lookout for suitable materials in garden centers. If you see a tile, slate, or slab that appeals to you, buy just one. Take it home and see how it looks before committing yourself to a truckload!

SEASIDE SANDBOX

Bring the seaside to your garden with this boat-shaped sandbox. A lid keeps the elements and inquisitive animals out, and there is provision for a parasol to be hoisted above the seat in very hot, sunny weather.

TOOLS

Pencil

Putty knife

1¼-inch (3-cm) flat drill bit

Electric sander

⅝-inch (16-mm) spade drill bit

Countersink bit

⅛-inch (3-mm) drill bit

Power drill/Screwdriver

C-clamp

Jigsaw

Tape measure

Crosscut saw

Miter saw or block

Combination square

sandbox lid

handle

seat

lid support

seat support

pipe insulation

side

comb

paddle

handle

base

MATERIALS

❖ Two 4 x 6-foot (1.2 x 1.8-m) sheets of plywood, ⅜ inch (1cm) thick

❖ 20 feet (6m) of stock 1⅛ x 5½ inch (2.5 x 14cm)

❖ Four 6-foot (1.8-m) lengths of stock, ¾ x 1½ inch (2 x 3.75cm)

❖ Four 6-foot (1.8-m) lengths of pressure-treated wood, 1⅛ x 2 inch (2.5 by 5cm)

❖ No. 6 Phillips-head screws, 1, 1¼, and 1½ inches (2.5, 3, and 3.75cm) long

❖ Plastic pipe 1¼ inches (3cm) diameter, 10 inches (25cm) long

❖ Foam pipe insulation, 1½ inches (3.75cm) in diameter, 15 feet (4.5m) long

❖ Quick-drying wood-colored filler

❖ Sandpaper

❖ Water-base wood stain in assorted colors

❖ Wood adhesive

❖ Nylon rope ⅝ inch (16mm) in diameter, 12 feet (3.6m) long

❖ Washed sandbox sand (play sand)

VARIATION

❖ Large pieces of scrap plywood

❖ Sandpaper

❖ Water-base wood stain

STARTING OUT - STEPS 1 TO 4

1 Mark a rectangle 36 by 66 inches (90 by 165cm) on one of the sheets of plywood. To make the "boat-shaped" end, measure and mark 18 inches (45cm) from the top. Measure and mark the midpoint on the top, then, using a long ruler or length of wood, draw a diagonal line from the midpoint to the marks on each side.

2 Raise and support the plywood above the ground using blocks of wood or flat stones. The plywood should be at least 4 inches (10cm) above the ground, so that the jigsaw blade can cut freely. Position the jigsaw blade on the waste side of the wood, and cut out the shape. You may have to reposition the supports as you cut.

3 To make the sides of the box, measure and mark two 33¾-inch (84-cm) lengths and two 48-inch (120-cm) lengths on the 1⅛-by-5½-inch (2.5-by-14-cm) stock. Draw a line across the wood at these marks, using your combination square to keep the lines straight. Hold the wood firmly on a suitable support and cut out each length with a jigsaw.

4 On each end of the longer lengths draw a line ½ inch (1.25cm) in from and parallel to the end. Along each of the lines mark three evenly spaced points. Drill a pilot hole at each mark, then countersink each one. Hold one of these lengths at right angles to one of the shorter pieces and fix them together with 1½-inches (3.75-cm) screws. Do the same to the other end. Now turn the structure over and screw the other length of wood into place.

SAFETY FIRST

Before using any power tools, always familiarize yourself with how they work. Make sure that the power cord is kept safely away from the working parts, and for additional safety, use a circuit-breaker in case you accidentally cut through the cord. Practice new or difficult cuts on a piece of scrap wood and only work on the stock for the project when you are confident of your ability. If you are not sure about using a particular tool, seek professional advice from an expert or ask someone who knows how to use it to help you.

PUTTING IT TOGETHER - STEPS 5 TO 8

5 Place the four sides on the base and draw a line along each of the inner edges: this marks the width of the sides on the base. Now place the base on top of the sides, leaving the end triangle overhanging. Drill and countersink a hole in each corner, then screw each corner to the base using 1½-inch (3.75-cm) screws. Continue drilling pilot holes and adding screws at roughly 4-inch (10-cm) intervals.

6 To make sides for the triangle of the base, set the blade of the jigsaw to a 45° angle and cut the end of a piece of 1⅛-by-5½-inch (2.5-by-14-cm) stock. Place this cut end on one of the corners of the box and make a mark that corresponds with the apex of the triangle. Draw a line at this mark with a combination square, then make another 45° cut along this line. Do the same for the other side of the triangle.

7 Drill and countersink two pilot holes at each end of one of the sides and at one end of the other—you only need one set of screws at the apex. Position the sides on the base and screw them into the sides of the rectangular box with 1½-inch (3.75-cm) screws. Then screw the apex together. Turn the sandbox over and screw through the base into the two sides, using 1½-inch (3.75-cm) screws and spacing them at 4-inch (10-cm) intervals.

8 To make the seat, measure the inside width of the box at the back of the boat shape. In this case, the measurement is 36 inches (90cm), but for accuracy, you should always measure your own. Cut a length of 1⅛-by-5½-inch (2.5-by-14-cm) stock to this length.

YOUR WORK SURFACE

An object as large as this will need to be made outside; a flat, paved patio area would be most suitable. You need a dry, flat, hard, level surface with an electric outlet nearby for power tools. Use wooden planks to raise the wood above the paving so that the wood can be drilled through without damaging the ends of the drill bits. If you have a portable workbench, use it to secure lengths of lumber as you drill or saw. If not, a sturdy stool or box and a set of C-clamps will do.

PUTTING IT TOGETHER - STEPS 9 TO 12

9 To make the seat supports, measure and mark 8 inches (20cm) on a length of ¾-by-1½-inch (2-by-3.75-cm) stock. Use a combination square to draw a diagonal line at 45° to this mark, so that the longest side of the wood to be cut is 8 inches (20cm). Cut along this line with a jigsaw. Cut out another 8-inch (20-cm) length in the same way.

10 Drill and countersink two holes 1½ inches (3.75cm) from each end of the seat support. To position the supports on the inside of the box, measure and mark a line 4 inches (10cm) up from the base on each side of the box. Position the top of the seat support on this line, so that the mitered edge is facing downward. Holding the support firmly, screw it into place with 1¼-inch (3-cm) screws.

11 For the parasol support, measure and mark the midpoint on one of the long sides of the seat, then measure 2 inches (5cm) up from this point. Hold the seat securely and drill a hole at this point using a 1¼-inch (3-cm) spade drill bit (see below).

12 Draw a line 8 inches (20cm) in from the back of the sandbox. Position the seat along this line, place the flat drill bit vertically in the hole, and push it down so its point makes a mark on the base. Take the seat away, raise the base on a piece of wood, then drill a hole through the base.

PROFESSIONAL TIP

Spade (flat) drill bits fit into any power drill and enable you to make large neat holes for doweling or other round shapes. The bit's end is flattened to the diameter of the hole with a sharp central point for precision location. They come in a range of sizes. Use an awl to make a hole first and place the bit's point in it, then hold the drill absolutely vertical and proceed as usual to drill the hole. No more than usual pressure is needed, but it is vital to keep the drill at 90° to the wood, or the parasol will slope off at an angle.

PUTTING IT TOGETHER – STEPS 13 TO 16

13 To secure the seat, drill and countersink two pilot holes 7¼ inches (17cm) and 4¼ inches (10.5cm) from each end and 1⅛ inches (3cm) down from the top of the sandbox. (Check that these holes are just above the seat support.) Place the seat on the supports, so that the front edge aligns with the top of the diagonal of each support. When in position, fix into place with 1½-inch (3.75-cm) screws.

14 Place a length of 1⅛-by-2-inch (2.5-by-5-cm) stock on each long side of the base to reinforce it. Make sure the ends are aligned, then secure them with 1½-inch (3.75-cm) screws, making sure that you screw into the sides of the box and not through the base. Secure two more lengths on the base, making sure they are evenly spaced and long enough to run to the front of the boat.

15 Using the side of the sandbox to guide the jigsaw, cut off the waste lengths of battens. Take extra care when doing this to cut as close as possible to the side of the boat without cutting into it.

16 To make the holes for the rope handles, turn the sandbox on its side and draw a line 2¼ inches (5.5cm) down from the top edge. On this line, mark six holes at 10, 19, 22, 31, 34, and 43 inches (25, 47.5, 55, 77.5, 85, and 107.5cm) from the end of the sandbox. Use a ⅝-inch (16-mm) spade drill bit and remember to clamp a piece of wood under each hole before drilling to prevent the wood from splitting. Repeat for the other side.

PROTECTING THE UNDERSIDE

Adding battens to the underside of the sandbox serves two important purposes. Sand and children are both heavy, and the battens help to strengthen the base, making it less likely to sag or buckle under their weight. In addition to this, the battens serve to lift the sandbox off the ground. This prevents the underside of the sandbox from resting on wet ground, allows air circulation, and lessens the likelihood of rot. Use pressure-treated wood battens, as these will also deter wood-eating bugs and beetles.

PUTTING IT TOGETHER - STEPS 17 TO 20

17 To make a support for the parasol, push the plastic pipe into the hole in the seat and down into the hole in the base. Mark with a pencil where the pipe meets the top of the seat. Pull the pipe out of the hole and cut along this line with the jigsaw. Push the pipe back into the seat—it should be flush with, or just below the seat. For safety's sake, make sure that there are no sharp edges on the plastic pipe.

18 You need to position the pipe insulation temporarily so that you can accurately measure the size of the lid. To cut the insulation, insert a utility knife into the top of the indented line that runs along the length of the insulation. Pull the knife slowly toward you to slit open the insulation.

19 Cut miters in the lagging to make neat corners. Place the insulation at the appropriate point in a miter saw, making sure that the slit you have cut is at the bottom. Hold the insulation steady and slowly cut a miter at the end.

20 Starting from the triangular point of the sandbox, pull the insulation apart along the slit and slide it onto one long side. When you reach the middle cross-section, use the utility knife to cut out a square to allow the insulation to fit over the cross-section.

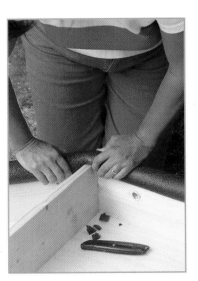

SOFTENING THE EDGES

Although it was not designed with this particular use in mind, foam pipe insulation really does provide a protective edging that is second to none. Its shape fits the wood well, it is easy to cut, and it is not only soft, but resilient and weatherproof too. Some children will always be bumping and scraping themselves, but by fitting this barrier you will certainly prevent at least a few of the minor accidents that inevitably arise in moments of high excitement. It also, incidentally, looks in keeping with the boat shape.

PUTTING IT TOGETHER – STEPS 21 TO 24

21 The lid of the sandbox overhangs slightly, so it will be slightly larger than the base. Lay the second sheet of plywood on a flat surface and place the sandbox upside-down on top of it. Trace around the sandbox holding a length of ¾-by-1½-inch (2-by-3.75-cm) stock between the sandbox and your pencil. Then cut out the lid with a jigsaw.

22 Now, using the lid as your guide, measure and cut out five lengths of ¾-by-1½-inch (2-by-3.75-cm) stock to go along each underside of the lid. Drill and countersink holes on these lengths of wood at regular intervals. Cut a miter where ends meet, or alternatively, you can leave a small gap. Secure the lengths of wood to the lid with 1-inch (2.5-cm) screws.

23 Drill holes for the rope handles on each side of the sandbox lid, using the ⅝-inch (16-mm) spade drill bit. Position the holes 2 inches (5cm) in from each side and 27 inches (67.5cm) and 36 inches (90cm) in from the back. Remove the pipe insulation from the sandbox and cover all the screws with filler. When this has dried, sand the whole box smooth, rounding off all the sharp edges.

24 Paint or stain the sandbox with a quick-drying, water-base wood stain or paint in bright colors on different parts of the sandbox. When the stain is dry, apply some wood adhesive to the tops of the sides of the box and press the pipe insulation onto it. To make the handles, thread rope through holes in the lid and in the sandbox and knot the ends.

CHOOSING SAND

When filling your sandbox, the best and most economical way to buy sand is from a large lumberyard, hardware store, or garden center. Ask for sandbox sand—sometimes called play sand—a washed sand sold in bags of varying weights. A sandbox needs to be generously filled to give the right kind of "beachy" feel, so buy a few extra bags if you are in doubt. Don't forget to always cover the sandbox when it is not in use because the sand will attract cats from miles around!

VARIATION - SANDBOX TOYS

1 Draw the outline of three paddles on a piece of scrap plywood. Make a template and trace the shapes, or draw them onto the plywood freehand. Hold the plywood firmly and use the jigsaw to cut these shapes out.

2 Make another template to draw the simple comb shape. Cut this out from plywood, as before. You can make the teeth of the comb pointed in the template if you wish—when you cut out the shape, you can then cut off the points.

3 When the shapes have been cut out, sand them down smooth, making sure that all the edges are rounded off.

4 Finally, using a quick-drying, water-based wood stain, paint each of the toys a bright color. You may need to apply several coats to achieve the desired effect, but remember to allow each coat to dry before starting the next.

MAKING TOYS

Playing in sand does not require elaborate equipment, and clues as to what is appropriate will come from observing your own child at play. If roadways are the choice, construct a simple pushing toy for a bulldozer; a wooden comb can simulate a plowed field and a paddle shape can be used to flatten the surface. Combs and paddles are simple shapes for which you can make your own templates. A broomstick can be cut up and used to sink holes, and wooden or thick-cardboard boxes make good molds for building walls.

PICNIC TABLE AND SEATS

Enjoy picnic meals in comfort with this versatile and easily transportable picnic table and seats. The beauty of this arrangement is that it does not involve any screws or bolts, but simply slots together for easy assembly.

TOOLS

Jigsaw

Tape measure

Pencil or felt pen

T-square

Paintbrush

Spirit level

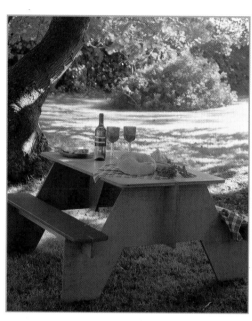

MATERIALS

❖ One 4 x 8-foot (1.2 x 2.4-m) sheet of exterior plywood, ¾ inch (2cm) thick

❖ Sandpaper

❖ Water-base wood stain in bright colors

❖ Clear varnish

table top

middle brace support

seat

side panel

seat support

NOTE

If you are an *experienced* woodworker, this project can be tackled without a workbench or clamps. Sawing on a toolbox or similar raised surface is fine. If you are *not* experienced, borrow a bench and clamps or have your lumber supplier cut your wood to size.

STARTING OUT – STEPS 1 TO 4

1 Use the templates given on pages 84–85 to mark your plans on the plywood. Find an area in your workshop or yard where you have enough room to lie the wood flat on the ground and still have enough space to move around as you draw. Start by drawing the first side panel.

2 Draw the second side panel. This will fit neatly next to the first. When drawing your cutting plan, make sure that you have a long enough ruler so that your lines are straight. A T-square is ideal, but if you do not have one, use a long steel ruler or a scrap piece of wood that is at least as long as the width of the plywood to ensure that your lines will be straight.

3 Next draw the middle brace support for the table. Using the full width of the plywood reduces the amount of measuring to be done, so there is less room for error. Take particular care when marking notches; make sure that they are measured accurately.

4 Now draw the two seat supports. Again, take care when marking the notches, as the stability of the table relies on these fitting together snugly.

MARKING AND CUTTING

Make your guide marks in pencil first, to allow you to either rub out or sand off any mistakes quickly and easily. If these guides are not clear enough, go over the lines with a felt pen when you are satisfied that you have marked each piece correctly. The pen marks will show up more clearly and help you when you start sawing the pieces. Though all the pieces of the table and seats are drawn on the plywood first, you may prefer to cut each piece as you draw it, so that your wood gradually becomes a more manageable size.

PUTTING IT TOGETHER – STEPS 5 TO 8

5 From the other end of the plywood sheet, measure 26 in (65cm). This rectangle will form the top of your picnic table. Then mark on the two 8-in (20-cm) wide rectangles for the seats.

6 Before you begin sawing, raise the plywood off the ground so that the jigsaw blade can move freely. Start by making the simplest, straight cuts for the table top and seats. If you have problems sawing in a straight line, clamp a scrap piece of straight-edged wood beside the cutting line to act as an additional guide.

7 Take extra care when cutting into the corners. It is possible to make a right-angled cut with a jigsaw: make a small cut in the wood past the corner, then gently curve the line of the blade back to join the straight edge. When you have cut out the piece, you can then straighten the corner.

8 For the sides and support braces you have to turn the jigsaw to cut the corners, as each shape butts up to another on the template. Pushing down on the jigsaw as you turn it will help you do this.

PLYWOOD

There are many different grades of plywood, and for this project you should choose exterior plywood. It is made with adhesives that will withstand all types of weather. Plywood tends to splinter at the edges when it is sawn, especially if you use a coarse-toothed saw blade. Avoid splintering by first scoring your cutting lines with a utility knife or use a fine-toothed saw blade. Use only downward strokes when sanding because an upward stroke could cause the top layer of the plywood to lift.

PUTTING IT TOGETHER - STEPS 9 TO 12

9 When you have cut out all the pieces, mark the position and depth of the slots. Take your time and measure accurately. If you wish, place a small scrap piece of plywood on its side and trace around the thickness of the wood as a guide for the width of the slots.

10 Cut the slots along the inside of your guidelines. As a general rule, always undercut—you can trim off more later. It is easier if you cut the two sides of the slot first and then curve your cut into the end of the slot. You will then have more room to move your blade, and you will be able to cut along the end of the slot easily.

11 Test that your slots are the correct width by pushing a scrap piece of plywood into the slot. If the fit is too tight, trim the slot by sanding it.

12 The table top fits into place over the middle brace support. Mark and cut your slots in the same way as before.

WATER-BASED STAINS

Water-based stains are, perhaps surprisingly, the better choice for wooden structures that are likely to live outdoors. This is because, in theory, if moisture gets into the wood and the coating is moisture vapor permeable, the moisture will be able to dry through the coating over the whole surface and not just at the point of entry. Water-based stains are, by their nature, quicker drying, lower in odor, and easier to clean up. They also emit fewer harmful solvent waste products into the environment.

PUTTING IT TOGETHER - STEPS 13 TO 16

13 Curved corners on a table top are very simple to create, and there is no chance of people hurting themselves on sharp corners. Find a cup or saucer that is about 4 inches (10cm) in diameter. Position this on the corner of the table and draw around it. Do the same on the other corners.

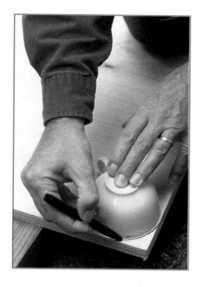

14 Using your jigsaw, carefully cut around the guides. You can also use this technique to round the corners on the seat benches if desired.

15 Sand all the rough edges. Wrap a piece of sandpaper around a small block of wood to give you a better grip, or use a sanding block. Make sure all the cut edges are sanded smooth.

16 To sand inside the slots, fold a piece of sandpaper over and pull it through the slots. Take your time to sand carefully; the end result will be much more appealing if all the edges are smooth.

USING A POWER SANDER

The biggest problem you are likely to face when using a power sander is removing more of the surface than you intended. It is easy to do, so practice beforehand on scrap wood to gauge the speed and efficiency of your sander. There are several types; the disk sander that fits a power drill is the most basic. The belt sander with a dust bag is the professional's choice. Sanders are easier to use if they have variable speed adjustments. Several grades of abrasives are available; for this job use a medium and a fine grade.

PUTTING IT TOGETHER – STEPS 17 TO 20

17 It is now time to assemble the table. It is a good idea to do this before you paint or varnish it so that any fine adjustments can be made. Start by fitting one of the side panels to the middle brace support.

18 Insert the other side panel. Your table is now freestanding. If you have trouble fitting the pieces together, resand the edges of the slots.

19 Fit the seat supports into position. These should fit snugly, as they not only add further support to the table, but also provide the bases on which the seats will rest.

20 Now fit the bench seats in place. These rest on the seat supports, providing a sturdy and stable seat.

MAKING ADJUSTMENTS

The table and seats are based on a slot mechanism, so having a tight fit is essential to the stability of the design. When you assemble it for the "test run" before painting, you may find the slots need slight adjustments to make the pieces fit easily. Don't reach for the saw, though; use sandpaper to smooth the pieces and ease them into place. Once you have taken apart and painted the pieces (be sure to coat the inside of the slots), rub candlewax along the slots before reassembly to help them glide easily into place.

FINISHING IT OFF – STEPS 21 TO 24

21 Check that the table top fits by slotting it in position. Use a carpenter's level to make sure that it is flat—a prerequisite for any table surface!

22 To prolong the life of your table and to make it more attractive, paint or varnish it. You will need to dismantle the table again before painting the various parts. Make sure you have a clean paintbrush as well as a few rags on hand to mop up any spills. If you wish to protect the surface you are working on, cover the ground with old newspaper, or a drop cloth.

23 Paint the bench seats in a colored wood stain. (See page 79.) Wood stains are supposed to be translucent so that you can see the grain of the wood through them. However, you can build up the intensity of the color by applying more layers of paint, without losing the effect. Make sure each coat of paint is completely dry before applying another layer.

24 Contrasting colors work very effectively on the table. However, you can pick any color scheme that suits your garden. Finally, add a coat of exterior-grade clear varnish over the finished paint, to further protect the table against the weather.

FURTHER PROTECTION

The corners of the side panels are the only part of this table that touch the ground. If you want to protect them from damp ground, cut a strip of roofing felt to the right length and tack it into place with panel pins. Alternatively, you can buy furniture feet from most hardware stores. Screw two of these on each side to lift the table off the ground. The disadvantage of these is that they can make the table wobble, so take extra care when positioning the table to make sure that it is on flat ground.

USING THE CUTTING DIAGRAM

You can cut the picnic table and seats from one sheet of 4-by-8-foot (1.2-by-2.4-m) plywood (see small diagram, above left). Note that the width of each slot is the same as the thickness of the plywood. The diagram has been enlarged here so that the measurements are easy to read. If you don't have enough room to draw and cut from one large sheet of plywood, ask your lumber supplier to cut it into smaller pieces. If you do ask someone to cut it for you, use the diagram to help you decide on the size of the pieces.

BRICK BARBECUE

A barbecue is a perfect way to enjoy a summer evening in the company of family and friends. This easy-to-make brick barbecue provides a permanent feature and focal point in a garden and will make socializing even more relaxing.

TOOLS

Bucket

Shovel

Hacksaw

Tape measure

Club hammer

Brick chisel

Carpenter's level

Bricklaying trowel

Awl

Gloves

warming shelf

ledge brick

grill shelf

extra decking

extra wall

slate hearth

MATERIALS

❖ Two wire grill shelves, 15½ x 26½ inches (39 x 66cm)

❖ 98 bricks

❖ Chalk

❖ Two 50-pound (22-kg) bags of soft sand

❖ Two 50-pound (22-kg) bags of masonry cement

❖ One slab of slate, 22¾ x 37 inches (57 x 92.5cm)

❖ Wooden decking, 20 x 20 inches (50 x 50cm), for the side worksurface

❖ String

❖ Steel wool

❖ Three brass cup hooks

NOTES

The barbecue will be a permanent feature of your garden, so you need to choose a suitable location. Site it in a cleared area away from anything that is likely to catch fire, preferably against an existing brick wall.

To ensure that it can be built in one day, choose an area with an existing hard surface. If you do not have a hard surface, create one by leveling out an area of soil and laying large paving stones on top, making sure that they are bedded well into the soil.

Always use gloves when working with cement, especially if you have sensitive skin.

STARTING OUT – STEPS 1 TO 4

1 Decide on a safe, practical position for the barbecue (see Note on page 86). Lay one of the wire grill shelves flat on the ground, then place the bricks along the back and each side, arranging them ½ inch (1.25cm) away from the shelf. Leave a gap of ½ inch (1.25cm) between each brick.

2 Carefully lift the grill shelf away and draw a chalk line about 1 inch (2.5cm) away from the outside edge of the bricks. Now take the bricks away, leaving the chalk lines to act as a guide when laying the first course of bricks (see tip box on page 91).

3 Now mix some mortar—always do this on a hard surface that can be washed down easily. If you do not have a suitable area, use a large sheet of plywood. Using your shovel as a measure, make a heap of nine shovelfuls of sand and three shovelfuls of masonry cement. Mix the two together, turning them over from one side to the other with your shovel until the mix is uniform in color.

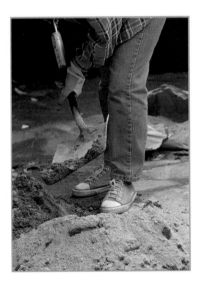

4 Make a well at the top of the dry mortar mix and half fill it with water. Using your shovel, push the dry mortar into the water. Lift and turn the mixture over with your shovel until the mortar has the consistency of thick cottage cheese (see below).

MIXING MORTAR

The mortar is mixed using the ratio one part cement to three parts sand, using your shovel as a measure. It is important not to add too much or too little water when mixing. To test that you have the right consistency, press the trowel into the mortar. If it leaves an impression when you take it away, then the mix is of the right consistency. If the shape simply oozes away there is too much water, so add some more sand. Alternatively, if the mortar cracks and crumbles, it is too dry and you will need to add more water.

PUTTING IT TOGETHER - STEPS 5 TO 8

5 Starting at one end, lay a trowelful of mortar on the ground between the chalk lines drawn in Step 2. Drag the trowel back through the mortar, wiggling it from side to side, to create a trough in the middle. (This will help the bonding of the bricks and ensures an even thickness of mortar.) Avoid laying mortar over the chalk line.

6 You are now ready to lay your first brick. Position it in the corner of the back row and push it down into the bed of mortar. Make sure it is in the middle of the chalk lines. When it is in place, tap it down firmly with your trowel.

7 Take another brick and apply mortar to the header (short) face. Push the tip of your trowel into the middle of the mortar to make an indentation. This helps the two bricks bond together.

8 Taking care not to let the mortar fall off the end, push this brick against the first brick and down into the mortar. Remember to keep it in the middle of the chalk lines on either side. Lift away any excess mortar squeezed from the joints as the bricks are pushed together (see below).

PROFESSIONAL TIP

Each time you spread mortar on the bricks, you will find that some drops off onto the ground. You will step in it if it is not cleared up, and spread it around the work area in no time at all! Get into the habit of picking up any loose mortar and scraping away the mortar that oozes out between the bricks as you are adding them. This can be lifted on the trowel and returned to the bucket or board to be reused. Keep an old dustpan and whiskbroom specially for outdoor work and use them to sweep away specks and splashes.

PUTTING IT TOGETHER - STEPS 9 TO 12

9 When you have completed the course of bricks at the back, check that they are level. It is important to establish a level from the start and to continue checking each course. Also, check that they are in line by holding the carpenter's level in front of the bricks. Tap with the trowel where necessary to correct their position.

10 When laying the side bricks, make sure that they are at right angles to the back. Use a combination square to check this angle. Tap the brick into place with your trowel and make sure it is secure in the mortar.

11 Lay the second course of bricks so that each brick is above a joint in the course below. This means that you need half a brick at each end. To cut a brick, lay it on a hard surface and position a brick chisel halfway across its stretcher (long) face. Hit the chisel with a club hammer. Turn the brick to another side and repeat until it breaks in half.

12 Be careful not to knock the brickwork as the barbecue walls grow taller. It will be unstable for about 24 hours, until the mortar has set. When laying the corner bricks, use the handle of your trowel to tap them into place, remembering to lift off any excess mortar with your trowel as you go.

BREAKING BRICKS

If you have the right equipment, bricks can be cut in half with surprising ease. A brick chisel is a strong, broad-bladed instrument with a short, thick handle, and a club hammer is a mallet that spreads the force of a blow along the full width of the chisel blade.

Score or mark the brick with the chisel where you want to make the cut. Put the brick on a flat surface and hold the chisel blade on the cutting line, with the handle slightly tilted. Hit the chisel with the club hammer and the brick will break cleanly in two.

PUTTING IT TOGETHER – STEPS 13 TO 16

13 Check that each course of bricks you lay is level. Place the carpenter's level vertically against the end, back, and sides of the brickwork, and tap the bricks gently into place. You should also check the interior width of your barbecue with your tape measure each time. Continue for six courses.

14 Lay the barbecue hearth on top of the sixth course of bricks to check its size. The slate for the hearth needs to completely cover the bricks at the back and sides (see below).

15 Lay a bed of mortar on top of the sixth course of bricks. With someone helping you, position the slate so that its front edge lines up with the front of each side wall. Once you have it in position, push it into the bed of mortar. Remove any excess mortar, then lay another course of mortar and bricks on top of the slate, in line with the courses below.

16 On the eighth course of bricks, you need to make ledges for the grill shelf by positioning two bricks on each side at right angles to the course. Lay the back row first, then position the first brick of a side wall so that a quarter of it overhangs the course at each side. Tap it into place with your trowel. Lay the next brick as usual, then finish the course with another ledge brick placed at a right angle.

PROFESSIONAL TIP

If you find it difficult to get hold of a large slab of slate that you can have cut to the desired size for your barbecue, a suitable alternative would be to use a large paving slab. The principal feature of whatever material you choose is that it should be able to resist heat and has to be able to hold the hot, burning coals without shattering or cracking. Slate and paving slabs are heat resistant and are especially well-suited because they can be hosed down for easy cleaning.

PUTTING IT TOGETHER – STEPS 17 TO 20

17 On the ninth course of bricks, lay two ledge bricks on each side of the barbecue and also one at the back. Make sure that the ledge bricks on the side are not directly over those in the course below. You will need to cut some bricks so that the courses are of equal length. On the final course of bricks, place one ledge brick on each side, above the ledge bricks on the eighth course, closest to the back.

18 To work out where to position the extra wall, lay the wooden decking on the ground, with one edge hard up against the side of the barbecue. Draw a chalk line at the opposite side of the decking. If you want an extra wall and decking shelf on both sides of the barbecue, repeat this on the other side.

19 The extra wall should be nine courses high, the same height as top of the first ledge brick on the barbecue. Because of the thickness of the slate, the top course needs to be thinner than the others. Using the technique in Step 11, you will have to cut the bricks *lengthwise* in the ninth course. Attach a length of string to the first course at the front of the barbecue, and use this to align the first brick of the extra wall.

20 Once the barbecue and the extra wall have been built, the mortar will be dry enough for you to tidy up the joints. Take a stick and gently drag it along the horizontal joints between the courses of bricks to make an indentation. Repeat for all the other joints, but be careful not to put any pressure on the walls. Finally, brush the walls and surrounding area clean.

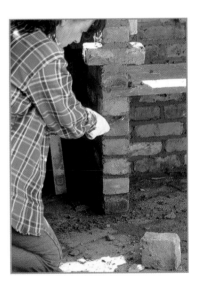

USING GUIDES

Before adding mortar, lay out a single course of bricks in the shape of your barbecue, allowing spaces for mortar between the bricks. Draw a chalk line to mark this position. This will help you to keep in line and make sure that both sides are of equal length for the first brick course. A length of string pulled taut between two bricks on a hard surface can be used to check the alignment of the two extending walls. Taut string forms a natural straight line that is easy to follow.

FINISHING IT OFF – STEPS 21 TO 24

21 The warming shelf (see diagram on page 86) should be narrower than the grill shelf, so that it won't get in the way of what's cooking underneath. Measure one of the grill shelves and mark the required depth. Hold the shelf firmly on some bricks or on a workbench and cut it with a hacksaw. Smooth the cut ends with steel wool, then rest the shelf on the top two ledge bricks.

22 Slot the grill shelf into position so that it is resting on the four lower ledge bricks. It should sit securely on these ledges, giving you a stable surface on which to cook.

23 Rest the decking on top of the wall and the corresponding ledge on the side of the barbecue. Remember that this is not securely fixed, so do take care when using the surface.

24 With an awl make three holes on the front edge of the decking. Screw a cup hook into each hole. You can hang your cooking utensils from these, so that they are within easy reach.

BARBECUING SAFELY

Build the fire toward the back two thirds of the slab so that there is no danger of hot embers falling out. Use proper long-handled barbecue tools to keep your arms clear of the heat. Keep a bucket of water nearby to damp down the fire if it becomes too hot. The coals should be left to burn for about half an hour before cooking begins, to give a more gentle, even heat that is less likely to cause fat to spit and flames to flare up. A wood fire is less predictable. As a precaution, keep a first aid kit handy while barbecuing.

TREE-TOP BIRDHOUSE

A birdhouse not only encourages birds into your garden, it also provides them with shelter when nesting. Make sure that the entry hole is not too large, or predators and larger birds may be able to get in and disturb a nesting pair.

TOOLS

1¼-inch (3-cm) spade drill bit

Small hammer

Screwdriver

Nail set

Power drill/ Screwdriver

Pencil

Paintbrush

Jigsaw or saw

Tape measure

Hammer

¾-inch (2-cm) drill bit

Combination square

MATERIALS

❖ Two 6-foot (1.8-m) lengths Dutch Profile tongue-and-groove boards

❖ Exterior wood adhesive

❖ Stock, ¾ x ¾-inch (2 x 2-cm) pine, 36 inches (90cm) long

❖ Finishing nails, ¾ inch (2cm) long

❖ Sandpaper

❖ One 12 x 48-inch (30 x 120-cm) pine shelf, ¾ inch (2cm) thick

❖ Nails, 1¼ and 2 inches (3 and 5cm) long

❖ Doweling, 12 inches (30cm) long, ½ inch (3.75cm) in diameter

❖ Quick-drying exterior matte varnish

❖ Hook and chain

VARIATION

❖ Sandpaper

❖ Water-base paint, gray and off-white

❖ Piece of 1⅛ x 5½-inch (2.5 x 14-cm) pine shelf, 28 inches (70cm) long

❖ ⅛-inch (3-mm) drill bit and No. 8 non-corrosive screws

❖ Weatherproof wood filler

❖ One 6-foot (1.8-m) length 2 x 2-inch (5 x 5-cm) pressure treated wood (see Note)

back wall

roof

side wall

perch

base

NOTE

If you make the variation, the end of the 6-foot (1.8-m) length of wood will be buried in the ground; so make sure you treat it with a suitable preservative.

STARTING OUT – STEPS 1 TO 4

1 Start by marking the lengths for the sides on a piece of tongue-and-groove. You need to measure, mark, and cut out four 10-inch (25-cm) lengths. You may find it easier to measure one length, then mark and cut this before marking the next ones; or you may prefer to mark them all and then cut them all together.

2 Next, mark lengths for the ends of your birdhouse. Measure six 8½-inch (21-cm) lengths of tongue-and-groove. Take care when measuring so that the pieces are all the same size and will fit together neatly.

3 Cut the tongue-and-groove along the lines you have drawn. If you are using a jigsaw, make sure that the lead is long enough to allow you freedom of movement.

4 To make the end pieces, apply a wavy line of wood adhesive in the groove of one of the 8½-inch (21-cm) lengths and slot the tongue of another into it. Add two more lengths in the same way, so that one end is made up of three pieces. Make the other end with the three remaining lengths. To make each of the side walls, glue two 10-inch (25-cm) pieces together in the same way. Leave the glue to dry.

LOCKABLE TAPE MEASURES

A lockable tape measure is an essential item, and enables you to measure and mark a length of wood on your own, since both hands are free. This kind of tape measure also has a mechanism to recall the end back into the casing. Many tape measures are calibrated in both imperial and metric measurements, which means there is less chance of making mistakes in any conversions. However, you should always stick to one set of measurements, either imperial or metric, throughout any one project.

PUTTING IT TOGETHER – STEPS 5 TO 8

5 When the glue has dried, mark and cut out the roof point on the two end pieces. To do this, first measure and mark the midpoint on one of the shorter sides. Then, you can either draw lines down to the sides at a 45° angle using a combination square, or measure 4¼ inches (10.5cm) down from the top on each side, and draw a line between the points and the midpoint. Cut out the roof point with a jigsaw or saw.

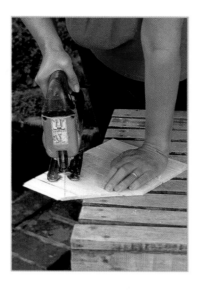

6 Measure the height of the sides of the end pieces. This is the length of the short side before the peak you have just cut. It should measure about 6 inches (15cm), but it is best to measure your own to be accurate. Compare this measurement to the height of the side pieces and trim them to fit, if necessary.

7 Working on the inside of one of the end pieces, hold an offcut of tongue-and-groove on its side along the edge of the end piece, then place a piece of batten right up against this. Draw a line along the edge of the batten. This shows you where to glue the batten. Repeat on the opposite side and on the other end piece. Trace two more batten widths along the roof sides, but do not use the tongue-and-groove width here.

8 Cut the batten to the required lengths. You need to miter the ends slightly so that all the roof supports will sit together snugly. Apply a wavy line of wood adhesive inside your guideline on one of the ends of the birdhouse. Place the batten in position close to your pencil mark so that the tongue-and-groove will fit alongside it. Repeat for the other three sides and the other end piece.

USING WOOD GLUE TO JOIN SURFACES

It is a mistake to think that the more glue you use, the better the adhesion you will achieve—this is simply not the case. In fact, wood glue contains water and as it dries the water evaporates. If you have used too thick a layer of glue, gaps will appear at this stage. So be sparing with your glue. In order to get the best results, apply an even, thin coating of glue to both surfaces to be joined. Then rub them together to create a suction between the two surfaces that encourages the bonding.

PUTTING IT TOGETHER - STEPS 9 TO 12

9 For extra strength, hammer finishing nails into the batten from the right side (the outside of the birdhouse). You will need about three nails for each side and two for each side of the roof, spaced evenly along the edges. Set the finishing nails so that their heads lie below the surface of the wood.

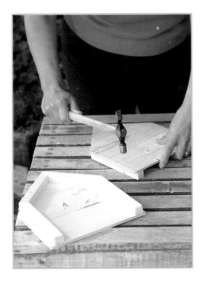

10 Mark the entry hole for the birds on one of the end panels. This should be centrally located about 5 inches (12.5cm) from the bottom. Place the marked piece on a block of wood or on a workbench, and drill the hole using the 1¼-inch (3-cm) drill bit. Mark and drill a ½-inch (1.25-cm) hole for the perch about 3 inches (7.5cm) from the bottom. Sand inside both holes (see below).

11 You are now ready to assemble your birdhouse. Apply a line of wood adhesive along the edge of one of the end pieces and fit it against a side panel. Hold in place for a minute or so until the adhesive "takes." Repeat on the other end and leave the glue to dry.

12 Now measure, mark, and cut out the roof from the pine shelf. One piece needs to be 8¼ by 12 inches (21 by 30cm) and the other slightly smaller at 7½ by 12 inches (19 by 30cm). The remainder of the pine shelf will form the base of your birdhouse.

PROFESSIONAL TIP

It can be awkward sanding inside the holes, especially if you do not have fingers that are long and thin! You may find it easier to find a piece of wood with roughly the same diameter as that of the hole. Wrap a piece of sandpaper around this and work it through the hole. A pencil is about the right diameter for the perch hole. For larger holes, use a length of doweling. Try to smooth the wood as much as possible so that the perch can be glued snugly into the hole. Pre-drilled holes only need slight sanding with fine sandpaper.

FINISHING IT OFF – STEPS 13 TO 16

13 Place the slightly smaller piece of roof on one of its longer sides, and apply a line of wood adhesive along the other edge. Glue the slightly larger roof piece to this so that the edges butt together. Hold for a few minutes while the glue "takes," then hammer about three evenly spaced 2-inch (5-cm) nails along the edge.

14 Position the roof on top of the birdhouse. Using your eyes as a guide, make sure there is an even distance at the front and back and glue into position. When the glue is dry, hammer nails into the supporting battens. Set the nails so that their heads lie below the surface of the wood.

15 To make the base, measure the bird house and add about 2 inches (5cm) to the length and width: cut out a piece of pine shelf this size. Center the house on the base and draw around it. Using a scrap piece of tongue-and-groove as a guide, mark where the batten goes along the inside of the side panels of the birdhouse. Cut two lengths of batten to fit and nail them into place.

16 Push a length of doweling through the small hole to make the perch. On the back, measure 3 inches (7.5cm) up from the bottom of the birdhouse and hammer a nail through to hold the perch in position. Paint the house with wood stain or varnish. When the paint has dried, place the house over the base and secure with glue and nails. Screw a hook into the middle of the roof to hang the birdhouse from a chain.

CENTERING OBJECTS ON A BASE

The easiest way of centering a square or rectangular object is to position it close to one edge of the base (say on the length of the base) on which you are working and measure the excess on the other side. Divide this measurement in half and draw a line at this point. Then position the object on another edge (on the width) and, once again, measure the excess. Halve this and draw a line at this point. Position one corner of your object at the point where the lines cross, and you will find that it is centered on the base.

VARIATION – FREESTANDING BIRDHOUSE

1 Make the birdhouse following Steps 1 to 16, but do not secure it to the base. After sanding the birdhouse and its base, paint both sides of the base. Turn the birdhouse upside down and paint under the eaves of the roof with gray water-base paint. Turn it up the right way and paint the perch, finishing with the top of the roof.

2 When this paint is dry, paint each side of the house with off-white water-base paint (see below), making sure you paint carefully around the base of the perch. When the paint is dry, secure the base to the birdhouse with wood adhesive and nails.

3 Copy the shape on page 110 onto the 1⅛-by-5½-inch (2.5-by-14-cm) wood, making each square 1 inch (2.5cm). Alternatively, you can design your own shaped bracket. Use the jigsaw to cut out four brackets, then sand each bracket smooth. Drill and countersink a hole in each of the vertical and horizontal arms of the brackets.

4 Position a bracket in the middle of the post so that its top is flush with the end and screw it into place. Fill the holes with filler, then paint the support. When the paint is dry, secure the birdhouse on the brackets by screwing up through the pilot holes in the horizontal arms of each support. Bury the end of the post about 18 inches (45cm) into the ground, or you can make extra supports to stand it up above the ground.

PAINTING THE BIRDHOUSE

An interior-quality paint is used to paint the birdhouse because, after exposure to the elements, it will show signs of weathering more quickly than an exterior paint. This will give the birdhouse a rustic look in a relatively short span of time. If you are not keen on a "weathered" birdhouse, you can either use an exterior paint or wood stain. If the color you want is only available as an interior paint, use it, but cover it with two or more coats of an exterior-quality varnish after the paint has dried.

RAISED HERB BED

A raised herb bed makes a fragrant and useful addition to any garden. Site it in an easily accessible place with plenty of natural light: ideally, beside a path and as close as possible to the kitchen.

TOOLS

Bucket

Pointing trowel

Bricklaying trowel

Combination square

Club hammer

Brick chisel

Float

Shovel

Carpenter's level

Tape measure

MATERIALS

- ❖ 128 used house bricks
- ❖ One 50-pound (22-kg) bag of gravel (coarse aggregate)
- ❖ One 50-pound (22-kg) bag each of Type 1A Portland cement and masonry cement
- ❖ Two 50-pound (22-kg) bag of clean, dry, finely-grained building sand
- ❖ Dishwashing detergent (see page 58)
- ❖ Terra-cotta tiles, whole or broken, at least 2 x 4 inches (5 x 10cm)
- ❖ Gravel
- ❖ Compost or loam
- ❖ Beach pebbles
- ❖ Potted herbs, such as rosemary, thyme, sage, chives, and oregano

tile creasing

corbeling

weep hole

NOTES

Cement is a skin irritant, so protect your hands with gloves while working with it, especially if you have sensitive skin.

To help you organize your time, read the tip box on page 104 before you start.

STARTING OUT – STEPS 1 TO 4

1 When you have chosen the position for your herb bed, clear a space 35 by 35 inches (87.5 by 87.5cm). The first task is to level the base. Dig down about 6 inches (15cm) and level the soil by dragging your spade backward and forward through it.

2 Once the base has been leveled, lay the bricks around the edge of the base. Leave a ½-inch (1.25-cm) gap between each brick; arrange them so that you do not need to cut any bricks to fit. This means that each subsequent course will also use whole bricks.

3 Push your spade into the soil on both sides of the bricks to mark their position. Remove the bricks and dig a trench where the bricks were, using the spade marks as a guide. The trench should be about 6 inches (15cm) deep, or roughly the depth of your spade. A square of earth will remain in the middle, which will help water drain from the herb bed.

4 Now mix the concrete for the foundations. Use your shovel as a measure and make a mound of 8 parts gravel, 3½ parts sand, and 2 parts Portland cement. Use the shovel to turn the gravel, sand, and cement over until they are mixed together thoroughly (see below). If you are mixing on pavement, remember to wash the concrete off as soon as you have finished with it.

MIXING CONCRETE

You need to make a stiff mix of concrete for the foundation, so be careful when adding water in Step 5. The concrete should only just fall off your shovel. Remember that you can always add more water, so start cautiously. The stiff mix means that bricks can be laid directly on top, before the concrete has set completely, enabling you to complete the building work of this project in a day (see page 104). If you add too much water, just add more ballast and cement in the same ratio as before.

PUTTING IT TOGETHER – STEPS 5 TO 8

5 Keep the mix in a mound and make a cavity in the middle. Add a little water to the cavity, push the top of the mix into the water, then continue to turn and mix in water. Add more water if necessary, but remember that it should be a stiff mix of concrete (see tip box on page 103).

6 Scoop the concrete into a bucket and sprinkle it evenly along the bottom of the trench. It needs to cover to a depth of at least 4 inches (10cm).

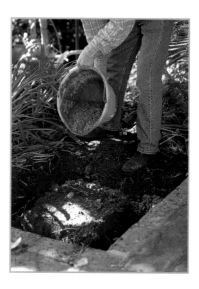

7 Use the float to spread the concrete around the trench. Hold the float on the surface of the concrete, patting and smoothing it down. You will probably need to compact the concrete down, as it will be quite stiff.

8 Now make some mortar. Use three parts of sand to one part masonry cement and turn the mix with your shovel until it is a uniform color. Add enough water so that the mortar just falls off your shovel. Working on one side at a time, load the bricklaying trowel with mortar, then let it slide off onto the trench foundations. Drag the trowel through the bed of mortar, moving it from side to side to create a jagged surface.

DRYING TIME FOR FOUNDATIONS

This is one project where we advise you to cheat a bit and spread your "day" over two weekends. The strongest foundations will be achieved by a slow drying process, so ideally you should split this project into two parts. The foundation concrete can be laid and covered with a plastic sheet until the actual brick laying is done some days later. Some settling will occur as the concrete dries and this could affect the wall's stability, so aim to get the foundations solid—and you will be making a garden feature to last a lifetime.

PUTTING IT TOGETHER – STEPS 9 TO 12

9 Starting at one corner, lay the first brick on the bed of mortar, pushing it down firmly. Add a layer of mortar to the header (short) face of the next brick. Push the tip of the trowel into the mortar to create an indentation, which helps the bricks bond. Butt the mortared end up against the laid brick, pushing it firmly into the bed of mortar.

10 Use a combination square to help you make the corners straight, using the handle of the trowel to tap the bricks into place. To lay the next layer, or course, place mortar on the laid bricks, then lay each brick of the next course over a joint in the course underneath (see box below).

11 On the fourth course of bricks, the first above ground level, you need to create weep holes (see tip box on page 106). This course is laid as before, except that you do not need to put mortar on the header faces of the middle brick on each of the sides of the herb bed. Remember to leave a gap at these joints—do not push the bricks hard up against each other.

12 To check that a wall is level, use a carpenter's level. Place it on top of the course of bricks and use the handle of your trowel to tap the bricks at the relevant points to maintain the horizontal level of the bricks.

PROFESSIONAL TIP

Bricklayers make building a wall look like child's play, but the rhythm of their work has built up over the years. As a novice, you will need to work slowly and carefully to achieve a neat result. Lay the first brick in the bed of mortar, then "butter" the end of the next one and butt it up against the first. Tap the end with the trowel handle and lay the next one. When you add the next course, the mortar will squeeze out below. Scrape it off with the trowel and return it to the rest of the mortar. Keep checking the wall with a carpenter's level.

PUTTING IT TOGETHER — STEPS 13 TO 16

13 On the fifth course, leave gaps on each side of the herb bed through which plants can grow. To do this, lay a corner brick, then leave a gap the size of one brick. Then lay another brick, pushing it into position and cleaning off any excess mortar with your trowel.

14 These large gaps are decorated with "tile creasings" (see diagram on page 102). The tiles need to be about 2 by 4 inches (5 by 10cm), with at least one straight edge. If you are unable to get tiles this size, you can break your own. Take a larger tile in your hand and use the edge of your trowel to break it up until you get the size required.

15 In the middle of the gap in the brickwork, lay some mortar, then lay the tile pieces, keeping the straight edge showing. Lay enough tiles to bring them level with the top of the bricks (about three tiles). Continue laying bricks, creating a gap on each of the sides and putting in the tiles.

16 On the next course, add a gap on each side, as before, but position the gaps so they are not directly above one another. Check that the walls are vertical with a carpenter's level. Use the handle of the trowel to tap it into a vertical position, making sure the walls are straight. Continue until you have six courses of bricks above the ground.

CREATING WEEP HOLES

Weep holes help water drain out of the herb bed. They are easily created by omitting mortar from the cross joints in the first course of bricks above ground. Without weep holes, the soil will easily become waterlogged, and whatever plants you have planted in your herb bed are sure to suffer. In an herb bed of the size used here, you need to have about six weep holes. If your herb bed is larger or smaller than the one made here, you will have to allow for more or fewer weep holes.

PUTTING IT TOGETHER – STEPS 17 TO 20

17 The final two courses of bricks are laid using a technique called corbeling. This is where the bricks overhang the course below. Lay a bed of mortar on the bricks, then a course of bricks as normal, except that the stretcher (longer) face should overhang the course below by about 1 inch (2.5cm). Position the first and last brick so that its side and end overlap the corner. Tap into place and remove any excess mortar.

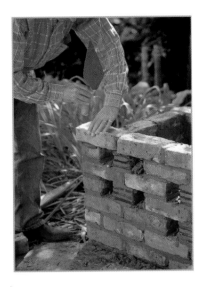

18 You will find, because of the overhang, you need a little more brick. Cut a brick to the required length by placing the brick chisel on top and hitting it hard with the club hammer until it breaks off. This piece can then be used to finish the course of corbel. Finish off by laying another course of corbel.

19 Leave the mortar to firm for about 30 minutes, then tidy up the joints. Hold the trowel diagonally on the mortar in a joint. Press down firmly and run it along the joint creating a diagonal face on the mortar. Repeat this in all the vertical and horizontal joints.

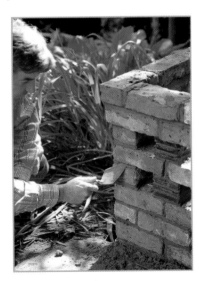

20 Use the pointing trowel to clear the excess mortar out of the weep holes. Brush the walls to remove any excess mortar. Now leave the mortar to set overnight before filling the bed with soil and planting the herbs.

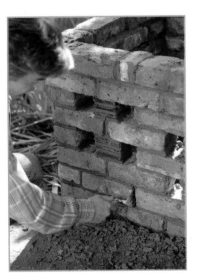

VARYING THE CORBELING

An imaginative approach to the corbeling on the herb bed can turn it into an even more strikingly decorative feature. Think of introducing different color bricks into the corbel, perhaps in alternation with the basic color or for the whole run. The mellow gray-yellow of old bricks could be contrasted with a dark-brown brick, for example. Alternatively, old glazed bricks will add an eye catching, luminous note to the structure, especially if the glaze has crackled with age.

PUTTING IT TOGETHER ~ STEPS 21 TO 24

21 Put a 2-inch (5-cm) layer of gravel across the bottom of the herb bed. Then start to fill the box up with compost until you are level with the openings in the brickwork. Take a small plant and push it into one of the openings, packing compost around it from the inside, so that it is firmly embedded in the gap.

22 Take a large piece of tile and place it against the back of the plant in the gap. Pack compost around this to hold it in place. The tile will stop the compost spilling out of the gaps.

23 Place pieces of tile behind the tile creasings, then pack compost behind them to hold them in place. You can also push beach pebbles into the gaps in the same way. Alternate between the tiles, pebbles, and plants on different courses of bricks.

24 When you have filled in all the gaps, finish filling the box with compost or loam. Plant the remaining herbs in the top of the bed.

CHOOSING PLANTS

Select herbs that enjoy a free-draining soil, such as the Mediterranean herbs: rosemary, thyme, marjoram, and oregano. A small bay tree, chives, fennel, and tarragon will give even more variety and culinary choice. (Avoid mint, because its roots may overtake the bed.)

The gaps can be filled with creeping varieties of thyme, wild strawberries, and helianthemums (rock roses), which will add color to the display even though they are not strictly herbs. You could also consider underplanting with bulbs for a spring display.

APPENDIX

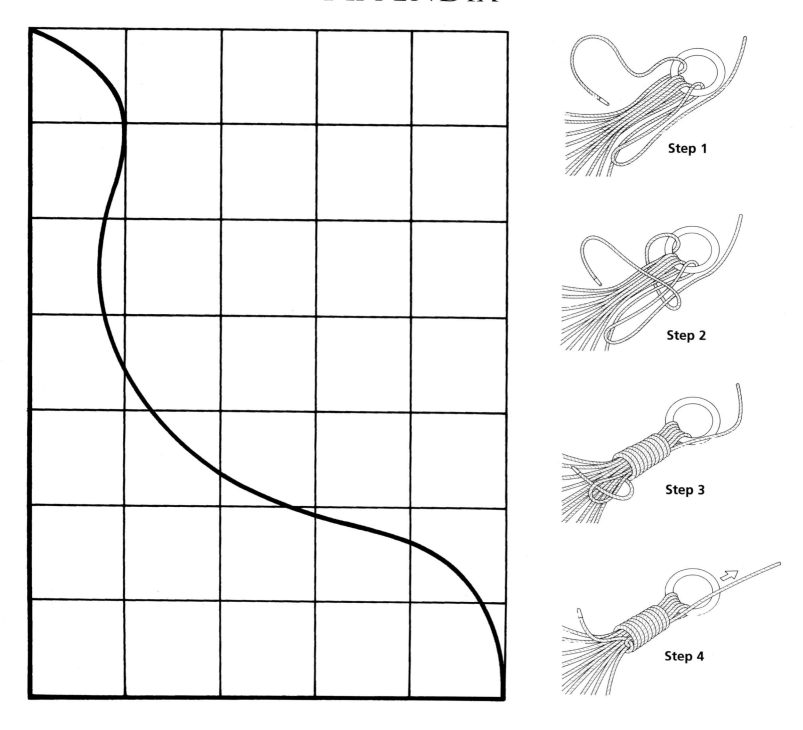

Step 1

Step 2

Step 3

Step 4

INDEX

GARDEN PROJECTS: *Acknowledgments*

The author would like to thank and acknowledge the hard work of the following people:

Sally Walton for being my wife; **Jack Howell** and **Paul Roberts** for their craftsmanship; **Stephanie Donaldson** for styling and allowing us into her home; and **Steve Differ** for always being there with a helping hand.

Marshall Editions would also like to thank **Sophie Sandy** for editorial assistance; **Joanna Stawartz** and **Philip Letsu** for design assistance; and a special thank you to **Deborah Grunfeld**, **Bronwen Davies**, and **Lisa Troni**, all of whom are indispensable.